MUSICAL FORM, FORMS & FORMENLEHRE

William E. Caplin
James Hepokoski
James Webster

Musical Form, Forms & Formenlehre

Three Methodological Reflections

Edited by Pieter Bergé

Leuven University Press

First edition (hardcover) published 2009
Second edition (revised paperback) published 2010

ISBN 978 90 5867 822 5

D/2010/1869/28

NUR: 663

Cover & book design: Jurgen Leemans

Contents

Preface

Ludwig Holtmeier

The present volume arose from a symposium on *Formenlehre* that took place at the 6th European Music Analysis Conference (EuroMAC) in Freiburg, Germany, October 10–14, 2007. The conference—with 'interpretation' serving as its overriding theme—was organized by the Deutsche Gesellschaft für Musiktheorie (this also being its seventh annual meeting), the Gesellschaft für Musik und Ästhetik, the Hochschule für Musik Freiburg, and the Freiburger Albert-Ludwigs-Universität (the conference occupying a central position within the 550th anniversary celebrations of that university). The conference was also supported by the Société française d'analyse musicale, the Gruppo analisi e teoria musicale, the Société belge d'analyse musicale, the Society for Music Analysis, and the Vereniging voor Muziektheorie (Dutch-Flemish Society for Music Theory). With 180 speakers and well over 500 participants, the 6th EuroMAC was, one must presume, the most comprehensive European conference on music theory ever.

The considerable success of the conference, which even surprised the organizers, seems to have been based on two main factors. In the first place, the content of the thematic sessions chosen jointly by the European societies ('Analysis and performance practice,' 'Text and music,' 'The interpretation of new music,' 'The notion of improvisation in the 18th century,' and '*Formenlehre*') seemed generally to have struck a chord. Moreover, most of the sessions that met with strong approval at the conference bore witness to some more or less clearly expressed national 'tendencies.' In Germany, the so-called *historische Satzlehre* (historically informed music theory) currently stands at the center of the music-theoretical mainstream, while that topic seems only recently to have gained ground in North American circles. By contrast, the Schenkerian sessions were dominated by North American theorists, yet were also complimented by some European specialists, a group that has been rapidly developing in the last number of years. In the second place, the theme of '*Formenlehre*' stood at the heart of the conference in a manner that seemed to transcend the ever perceptible departmentalization of national customs and discourses within European music theory as well as the rift between North American and European research and pedagogical traditions. Music-theoretical discourse on *Formenlehre* is a truly international one: it is currently perhaps the only discourse, within the context of a 'global' music theory, that rests on a broad foundation, anchored by various national traditions.

Our conscious effort to build bridges with North American music theory was met by some critical concerns in the run-up to the conference. A few of my European colleagues required an explanation for our having invited one Canadian and two American scholars to discuss one of the most 'German' of all theory topics at a plenary session right in the heart of this large European conference. Was it possible that something was being sold as 'new' that was already standard practice throughout Europe and, especially, Germany? Mild resentments arose every now and then, but also a rarely admitted feeling of inferiority in the face of a music-theoretical tradition whose superior productivity since the end of the Second World War is widely perceived and recognized, but whose specific form and content remain even today somewhat foreign to many European music theorists. Nevertheless, the meeting of cultures at the Freiburg conference was an extraordinary success, because the *Formenlehre* topic could be discussed on equal footing, face-to-face. More simply put: beyond all the secret codes and closed systems, a language was spoken here that was familiar to nearly all the participants. In the course of this amicable and open meeting in Freiburg, even isolated, critical reservations gave way to insights. Thus, the three scholars whose differing ideas are documented in this volume stood at the center of the Freiburg conference *not* as representatives of North American music theory, but as those who, in recent years, have considerably determined the international discourse on *Formenlehre*. A European conference on music theory is first of all a *music theory* conference, and only thereafter *European*.

I expressly thank William E. Caplin, James Hepokoski and James Webster, but also especially Pieter Bergé for his conceiving and organizing the Freiburg *Formenlehre* session and for his efforts in bringing it to publication.

Ludwig Holtmeier – Freiburg im Breisgau, October 2008

Prologue
Considering Musical Form, Forms and Formenlehre

Pieter Bergé

Defining the concept of 'musical form' is a precarious enterprise. Many musicologists and theorists have undertaken it and have inevitably confronted the question, what *is* musical form? In most cases, however, this central question does not persist for long. Often, it is evaded almost immediately and rephrased as a question (or group of questions) that tries to circumscribe how musical form is *generated*, how it is *constituted*, how it *functions*, and so forth. In the essays presented in this volume, a similar shift can be observed more than once. William E. Caplin, for instance, launches his essay "What Are Formal Functions?" with the question, "what is form?" [>21].[1] Quickly thereafter, however, he undertakes the exercise of listing "terms and expressions associated with *discourse about* form in music" [>21, my italics]. The list is impressively long and contains a series of terms that open up fascinating perspectives on how to approach form [>see Caplin's Figure 1.1, 22]. Soon enough, however, Caplin admits that he will deliberately avoid providing anything like a "dictionary definition" of form in music, stating that a "more *effective* (...) approach" might be to "consider (...) the sorts of things we typically *do* when analyzing form in connection with *a specific work*" [>23, my italics]. In other words, the general question about the very identity of musical form is rapidly abandoned in favor of a potentially infinite list of more practical and concrete investigations.

James Hepokoski also poses the question, "what is 'form' itself?" at the onset of his essay "Sonata Theory and Dialogic Form," and thereby firmly states that it is "[T]he most basic question at stake when we deal with our own concretizations of musical structure or when we seek to build systems of formal classifications" [>71]. In addressing this key question, however, Hepokoski almost immediately proceeds to "single out two of its basis principles" [>71]. First, he notes that the perception of form is essentially "a collaborative enterprise" [>71], and secondly he suggests that "the full range of an implicit musical form" only reveals itself in "a dialogical process" between the specific composition itself and its broader generic context [>71]. However crucial these principles may be—and they are indeed!—the question "what *is* musical form?" is in some way deflected to an exposition of *some* of its essential characteristics. Although the meaning of a concept fundamentally relies, of course, on the definition of these qualities, it is evident that the essence of the defined concept itself does not coincide with them. Like Caplin's approach—though in a different manner—Hepokoski's implicit understanding of what form *is* thus precedes the further characterization of its identity.

James Webster, in his essay "*Formenlehre* in Theory and Practice," approaches the case in a somewhat different, but still comparable, way. Webster 'skips over' the definitional question and jumps right into its multifarious characterizations. He starts "by briefly discussing two important general issues *affecting* musical form" [> 123, my italics]. In his approach, a concept of form is, so to speak, presupposed—which does not imply that a clear definition of 'form' is at hand as an *a priori* certainty, of course. Rather, the negation of the question seems to suggest its relative irrelevance for the real scope of Webster's interest: the practice of musical analysis.

In these contexts, to 'digress from' or to 'skip over' the question "what *is* musical form?" should by no means be considered as a failure. Apart from strongly indicating the complexity of the phenomenon itself, this definitional omission represents a general intention to grasp musical form within a theory or method that reveals only *aspects* of form; these aspects are then considered to be crucial for its identity, as well as relevant for the concrete praxis of musical analysis. Inevitably, however, such an approach implies the necessity of defining a well-circumscribed theoretical perspective that both explains and justifies the constraints implied in the proposed model. Therefore, the three analytical viewpoints presented in this volume depend, irrespective of whether they should be regarded as 'theories' or 'methods,' on the inner coherence of their methodologies. To define these methodologies, rather than to define what musical form *is*, remains the true ambition of this volume. To its contributors, it offers a unique opportunity to articulate the essentials of their approaches to musical form, to clarify their unique (but, of course, not unrelated) position in the realm of so-called *Formenlehre*, and to confront their interpretations with the differing opinions of their colleagues.[2]

William E. Caplin's essay is primarily conceived as a theoretical reflection on his basic concept of 'formal function.' Starting from what he himself considers to be a lacuna in his well-known treatise *Classical Form* from 1998,[3] Caplin sets out to elucidate this concept and to adduce arguments for why his 'theory of form' is essentially a theory of 'formal *functions*' rather than of 'formal types,' or of 'form' in general. By focusing on the theoretical and methodological basis of his analytical system, Caplin offers an appendix to his theory, albeit one that from now on should rather be considered its proper *preambulum*. As such, it surely will clear up some of the misunderstandings his theory has provoked in the past decade and make more conscious its essentially rigorous and highly systematic way of approaching classical form.

James Hepokoski's essay focuses on the concept of 'dialogic form.' This idea had already been introduced in his earlier writings, both in discussing specific formal phenomena[4] and in the general presentation of his and Warren Darcy's Sonata Theory.[5] In the reception of Sonata Theory, however, most discussions have concentrated on the entire network of compositional options laid out by its authors, especially focusing on some of its most challenging concepts (such as 'medial caesura' and 'essential expositional closure'). As a result, the fundamental role 'dialogic form' plays in their theory has largely been underrated, if not fully neglected. 'Dialogic form' is not, however, just another 'characteristic' of form. On the contrary, "the deeper sense of form," as Hepokoski puts it [>72], is implied in the dialogical status of form itself. His essay in this volume should therefore be considered a vigorous attempt to reconfirm the essentially *contextual* basis of Sonata Theory, and, by extension, of all theories of form that operate within a normative framework.

James Webster's position again differs somewhat from that of his colleagues. The most obvious contrast, of course, is that Webster has never published a 'theory' of musical form and—more importantly—has never aspired to develop one. He repudiates the constraints that, according to him, are inevitably implied in the construction of such a theory. From his point of view, theories of form tend to include hierarchical structures that privilege some parameters over others. To overcome this analytical one-sidedness, Webster advocates a 'method' rather than a 'theory,' and parametric 'multivalence' rather than parametric 'constraint.' He urges analysts of musical form to integrate in their formal interpretations all parameters that, in some way or another, affect the constitution of a specific work. He invites them not to invent models to collocate similar compositions, but to concentrate on the uniqueness of each work by attending to the particularity of how all active parameters relate to each other in a single piece.

Webster's approach is not completely new, of course: it belongs to a long tradition initiated by Donald Francis Tovey and carried on by many others throughout the twentieth century.[6] However, with the emergence of the comprehensive 'theories' by Caplin, on the one hand, and Hepokoski and Darcy, on the other, the 'method' of multivalent analysis gains in interest as an alternative approach. As a matter of fact, the concept of 'multivalent analysis' is fundamentally irreconcilable with the ambition to construct any kind of 'theory' of musical form. The confrontation of 'theory' and 'method' thus provokes—here, as well as in a broader theoretical perspective—further investigations into the fundamentals of analyzing musical form. To be sure, varying *theories* of musical form—those that start from different assumptions and definitions—inevitably generate conflict among themselves. And whereas such theories may well share a belief in the relevance and feasibility of a coherent and systematically applicable model, this commonality of intent will not prevent them from disagreeing on fundamental points of methodology and content.

The exhilarating tension between 'different theories,' or between 'theories' and 'methods,' forms the basis of the structural layout of *Musical Form, Forms & Formenlehre.* The volume is divided into three parts. Each part begins with an essay in which one of the authors explains and elaborates his fundamental concerns about musical form. Part I deals with Caplin's concept of 'formal functions'; part II concentrates on Hepokoski's idea of 'dialogic form'; part III is based on James Webster's plea for 'multivalent analysis.' After each opening essay, the two opposing authors comment on issues and analyses they consider to be problematic, underdeveloped, or overemphasized. Their remarks largely adhere to issues brought up in the essays presented here and are cast in a style that ranges from the gently critical to the overtly polemical. Finally, in the concluding section of each part, the author of the initial essay is given the opportunity to reply to those comments and, eventually, to rebut them. Needless to say, this structure does not lead to—nor does it envisage—general consensus; rather, the 'dialogic' pattern underlying the organization of this volume is intended to encourage the clarification of fundamental *differences*. If this work succeeds in adequately distinguishing the methodologies advocated by Caplin, Hepokoski and Webster, and if it has challenged these authors to refine their basic views on musical form, it will have fulfilled its initial promise. If, in addition, it provokes its readers to investigate the extent to which these methodologies (as dissimilar as they may be) can bear upon their own attempts to grasp the multi-layered essence of musical form, this would gladly be welcomed as a satisfactory and salutary bonus.

The decision to compile this volume was taken immediately after the plenary session 'Considering Musical Form, Forms & *Formenlehre*' at the European Music Analysis Conference in Freiburg, in the late afternoon of Friday, October 12, 2007. This session consisted of a short introduction by the editor of this book, three lectures (successively by James Hepokoski, James Webster, and William E. Caplin) and a plenary discussion, chaired by L. Poundie Burstein. Soon after the three protagonists of the session had started to revise their lectures for publication, the idea arose to expand the discussion part and to create a format in which a lively and reciprocal confrontation of competing points of view would become possible. I want to express my gratitude to the three authors of this book, who were immediately prepared to jump into this challenging adventure without any reservations. Sure enough, the *Essays* and the *Comments* assembled here sometimes provoked reactions of astonishment, annoyance and even irritation; and the *Responses* were surely not conceived to draw a veil over all discrepancies and antinomies that emerged in the debates. But during the whole process, the authors have shown great discernment and intellectual dignity in their urge to present and defend their own fundamental ideas on musical form. Without their having sustained that demanding attitude, the present volume could never have been realized in its present form.

I am also grateful to Ludwig Holtmeier, chair of the Sixth EuroMAC-conference, who, from the very beginning, warmly encouraged and supported the organization of the *Formenlehre* session in Freiburg. He also provided the financial means that were needed to make this event possible. Furthermore, his proposal to schedule the lectures and discussions as a plenary session was, for all involved, a unique privilege, one that undoubtedly enhanced its attraction and impact.

Finally, I wish to express my gratitude to those who have been helpful in the editing of this book: L. Poundie Burstein, for co-preparing and co-leading the plenary discussion, in which a number of issues were raised that are developed further in the present volume; Steven Vande Moortele, for his much appreciated 'second opinions' and his willingness to comment uninhibitedly on earlier versions of the texts; Markus Neuwirth, for his multiple proof-readings and careful preparation of some of the music examples; and Marike Schipper, Director of Leuven University Press, for her empathy and flexibility in creating the best possible conditions for editing and designing this book.

Notes

1. Page numbers in square brackets refer to pages in the present volume.

2. The German word '[musikalische] Formenlehre' literally means 'theory of [musical] forms.' As a concept, it refers mainly to the nineteenth- and twentieth-century German tradition of publications in which all standard musical forms within the tradition of Western music are systematically represented and discussed. The third volume of Adolph Bernhard Marx's *Die Lehre von der Musikalischen Composition* (Leipzig, 1837–47) counts as one of the earliest reference works. Later publications within the same tradition include Hugo Riemann's *Katechismus der Kompositionslehre (Musikalische Formenlehre)* (Leipzig, 1889), Hugo Leichtentritts *Musikalische Formenlehre* (Leipzig, 1911; published in the United States in 1951 as *Musical Form*), and literally dozens of textbooks with the same or a similar title. A more recent example is Clemens Kühn's *Formenlehre der Musik*, released in 1987, and still very much used in Germany today. One of the more influential books in this tradition – and actually more a 'study' than a conventional 'treatise' – is Erwin Ratz's *Einführung in die musikalische Formenlehre*, especially its third edition (1973). Of particular interest for the reception of *Formenlehre* in North America is Arnold Schoenberg's posthumously published *Fundamentals of Musical Composition* (ed. Gerald Strang & Leonard Stein, 1967). In current North American music theory, *Formenlehre* is mainly linked with the study of forms in the instrumental music from the (Viennese) classical period and the romantic era.

3. William E. Caplin, *Classical Form. A Theory of Formal Functions for the Instrumental Music of Haydn, Mozart, and Beethoven* (1998).

4. E.g., James Hepokoski, "Back and Forth from Egmont" (2001).

5. James Hepokoski & Warren Darcy, *Elements of Sonata Theory. Norms, Types, and Deformations in the Late-Eighteenth-Century Sonata* (2006).

6. Caplin, and Hepokoski & Darcy, also have their historical 'ancestors.' In the *Preface* to *Classical Form*, Caplin acknowledges that the 'origins' of his theory of formal functions go back to "a seminar on musical form given by Carl Dahlhaus at the Berlin Technical University [in 1978] in which the principal reference work was Erwin Ratz's *Einführung in die musikalische Formenlehre*" (*Classical Form*, vii). Hepokoski & Darcy in their *Preface* insist that Sonata Theory is "a *fresh* approach to one of the most familiar topics in the field of music" (*Elements of Sonata Theory*, p. v, my italics); nevertheless, they remain "in dialogue with the several current approaches to this subject" as well as with "the theoretical discussions of eighteenth- and early-nineteenth-century writers" (ibid.)

PART I
William E. Caplin

&

THE THEORY OF FORMAL FUNCTIONS

What Are Formal Functions?

William E. Caplin

The question posed in the title of this essay should, by all rights, have been answered in my treatise *Classical Form: A Theory of Formal Functions for the Instrumental Music of Haydn, Mozart, and Beethoven*.[1] Yet in a number of respects, this study did not sufficiently address the central concept of my *Formenlehre*. Indeed, I toyed with the idea of writing a summational chapter on general notions of formal functionality; but, to be frank, I was exhausted with the project after working on it for many years, and, more importantly, I was aware that I had still not adequately developed the idea. In fact, it was only in the process of writing the glossary of terms that I realized my difficulties in providing a satisfactory definition.[2] In the intervening years, I have given considerable thought to what constitutes the concept of formal function, and the following essay begins to explore some of these ideas.

Before proceeding further, however, let me survey various meanings associated with the general notion of musical form, with the goal of eventually situating my own theory of formal functions within the semantic range expressed by that broad term. A number of years ago, I brainstormed the question 'what is form?' with a group of graduate students. Figure 1.1 summarizes our discussion as a list of terms and expressions associated with discourse about form in music. Form, it seems, involves highly general concepts, such as organization, structure, patterning, and the only somewhat less abstract notions of process, function, hierarchy, etc. A theory of form in general typically proposes a set of specific forms (in the plural), such as song form, sonata form, rondo form, and concerto form. And these formal types often relate to various genres of music from any number of style periods. In connection with a given form, we often speak of its constituent parts using terms such as phrase, idea, statement, repetition, sequence, and section. As well, discussions about form invariably implicate ancillary parameters, such as motive, melody, cadence, harmony, rhythm, and

FORM

GENERALITIES

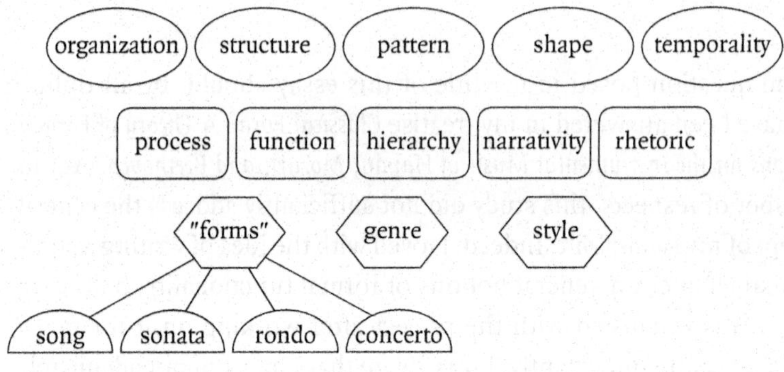

PARTS OF FORM

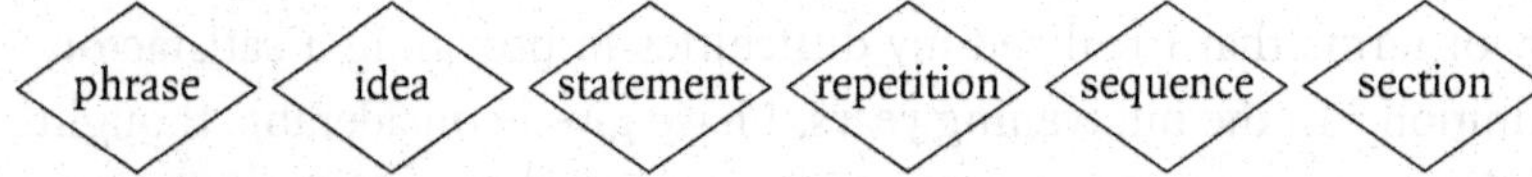

ANCILLARY PARAMETERS

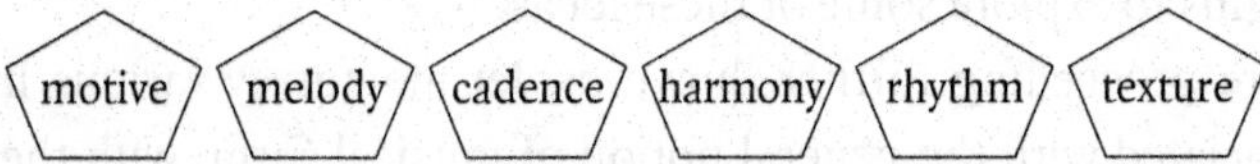

BINARY OPPOSITIONS

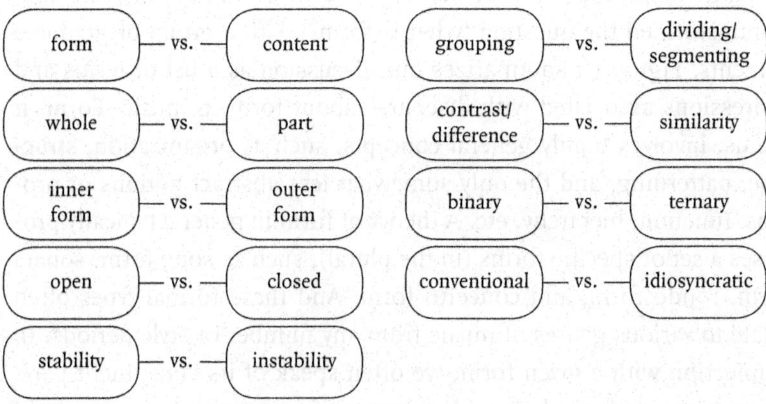

Figure 1.1 Terms associated with 'musical form'

texture. Finally, when talking about form, there arise a large number of binary oppositions, over which much ink has been spilt: form vs. content; grouping vs. dividing; whole vs. part; contrast vs. similarity; inner form vs. outer form; binary vs. ternary; and so forth. Such oppositions reflect the difficulties theorists often have in conceptualizing form and sorting out its manifold meanings.

So far, I have avoided providing anything like a dictionary definition of form in music. Rather, I think we might more effectively approach the issue by considering the sorts of things we typically do when analyzing form in connection with a specific work, say, the opening movement of Beethoven's First Symphony (see Figure 1.2). Most descriptions of form begin by segmenting the music into distinct and contiguous time-spans at multiple levels in a structural hierarchy.[3] We can consider this tree-like representation to be an analysis of the work's 'grouping structure,' with the notion of grouping relating to our cognitive ability to 'chunk' (as psychologists like to say) the music into discrete units of time.[4] Next, we normally want to indicate how these time-spans relate to each other beyond their purely hierarchical connections (as shown by the lines linking the boxes). Many traditional theories of form use letter schemes to show commonalities of 'thematic content' among the groups. Our figure presents a partial attempt along these lines. At each hierarchical level, I have used letters, starting with *a*, to show similar materials based on melody, motive, texture, and the like.[5]

The primary weakness of such a letter-based analysis, however, is that it fails to represent in any explicit manner what I, along with many others, consider to be a fundamental aspect of form—namely its intimate association with musical 'temporality.' Central to our experience of time in general is our ability to perceive that something is beginning, that we are in the middle of something, and that something has ended. To these general temporal functions, we can add the framing functions of something occurring before-the-beginning or after-the-end. Musical form directly engages our temporal experience of a work inasmuch as its constituent time-spans have the capacity to express their own location within musical time. In some sense, the idea that a given span has a temporal function issues automatically from the hierarchical structure we are already considering. As Figure 1.3 shows, for a given time-span

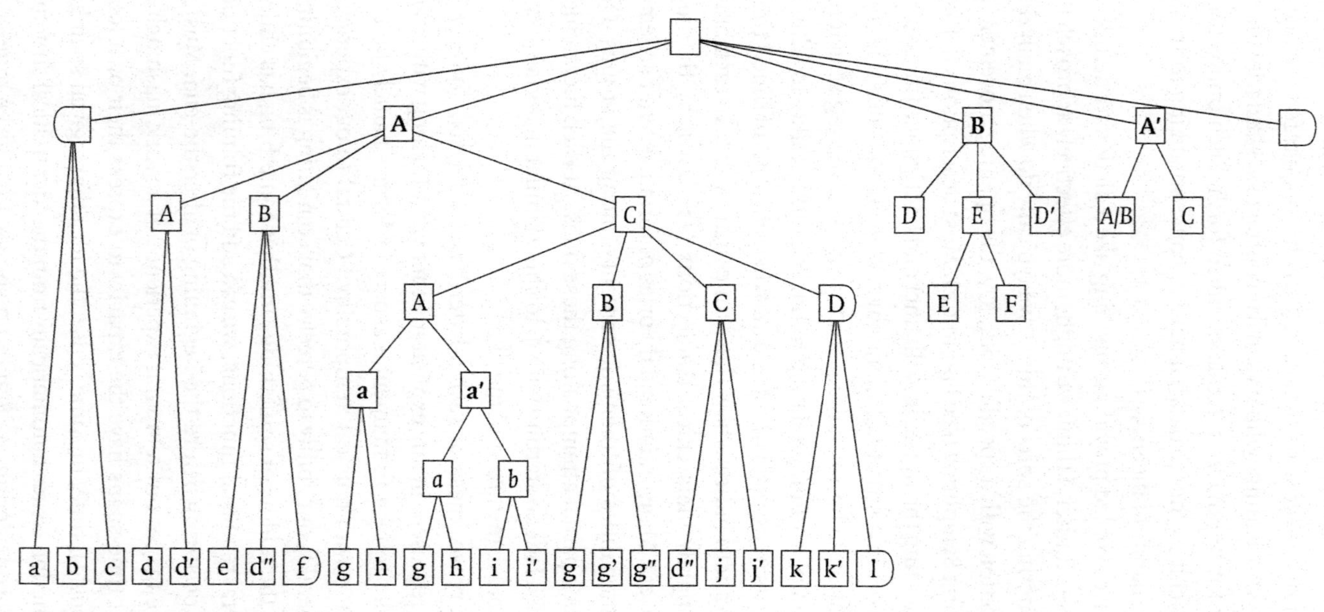

Figure 1.2 Ludwig van Beethoven, Symphony No. 1, Op. 21, i: grouping structure

at one level of structure, any one of its constituent 'lower-level' spans could be understood, very generally, as a beginning, middle, or end of that 'higher-level' span. This figure reflects what Kofi Agawu has called the 'beginning-middle-end' paradigm of introversive semiosis.[6] Though rather crude, this representation has the advantage of revealing that each time-span at the surface of the piece has a unique temporal character. Take, for example, mm. 77–80 (circled). This passage can be understood, moving from the surface to the background, that is, from bottom to top, as the 'beginning,' of the 'middle,' of the 'end,' of the 'beginning,' of the entire movement. I would suggest that a composer's ability to realize in a convincing manner these kinds of temporal multiplicities accounts for experienced listeners (that is, those who are familiar with the host of compositional conventions informing this style) being able to discern quickly just where a particular passage lies within the overall temporal extent of a work.[7]

What makes the analysis in Figure 1.3 so crude, of course, is that the temporal functions at different levels of formal organization are considerably more diverse than the simple labels 'beginning,' 'middle,' and 'end' would suggest. And it is precisely the attempt to differentiate just how such spans express their temporality that is the goal of a theory of formal functions, the particular kind of formal theory that I espouse. Inspired by Arnold Schoenberg and his students, especially Erwin Ratz, I have systematically defined a variety of formal functions operating at multiple levels in a work.[8] Figure 1.4 shows such a form-functional analysis, though even other, more surface-level functions are not identified here, such as 'basic ideas,' 'contrasting ideas,' 'codettas,' etc. The specific form-functional categories of Figure 1.4 are manifestations of the generalized temporal functions of Figure 1.3, and, as I will discuss later, each formal function arises from criteria involving multiple parameters, most importantly harmony, tonality, grouping, and cadence.

Let me summarize a number of these functions. (Of course, many of these are familiar from the traditional *Formenlehre*.) At the top of the hierarchy, we observe the five broad formal functions of the overarching sonata form: the slow introduction, a before-the-beginning; the exposition, an initiation; the development, a medial function; the recapitulation, an ending; and the coda, an after-the-end function. Within

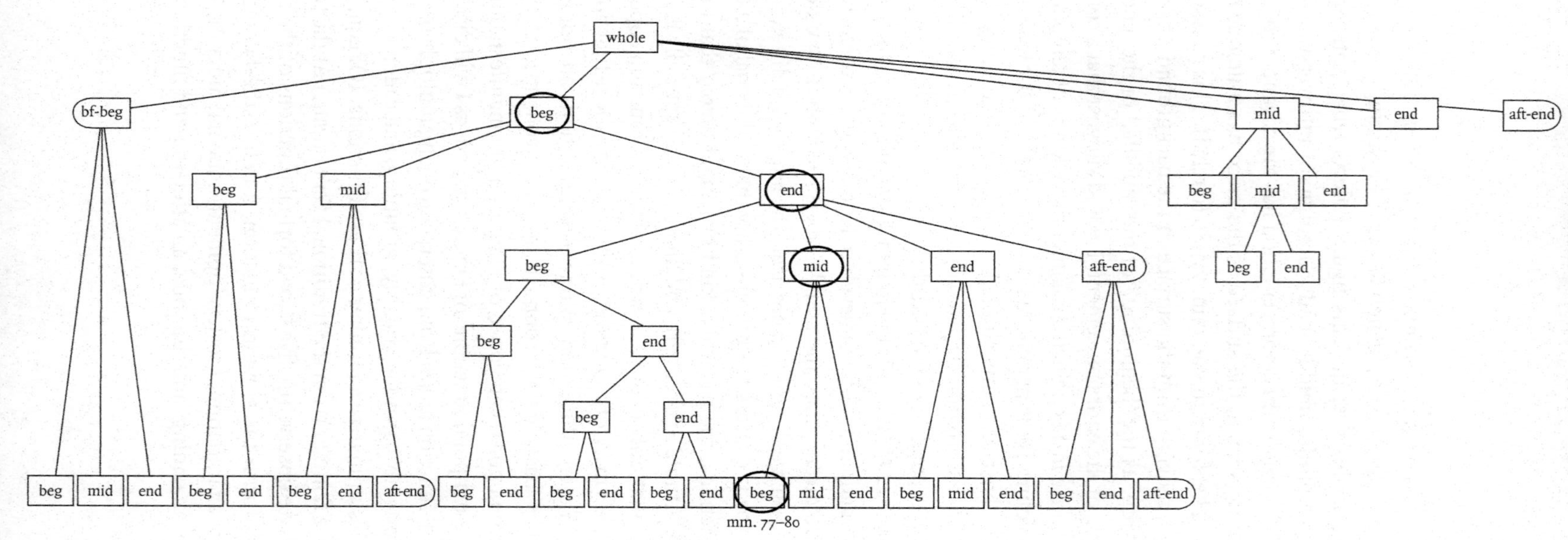

Figure 1.3 Ludwig van Beethoven, Symphony No. 1, Op. 21, i: temporal functions

the exposition, we recognize the initiating function of main theme; the medial function of transition; and the ending function of subordinate theme.[9] In the case of the first movement of Beethoven's Symphony No. 1, a group of three subordinate themes together constitutes the exposition's ending.[10] And following the last of these themes, a brief closing section functions as an after-the-end of that theme. Within the unit labeled 'subordinate theme 3' reside the three functions—presentation, continuation, and cadential—that make up what Schoenberg first identified as a sentence (*Satz*), a theme-type that plays perhaps the most prominent role in all of classical phrase structure. And in 'subordinate theme 1,' we see an initiating antecedent and a closing consequent, which together make up the period form. Notice that the period contains only two functions: a specific medial function does not arise in this theme-type.

When talking about the expositional functions of main theme, transition, and subordinate theme, it may strike the reader as odd that I refer to the latter, in this case a group of three subordinate themes, as the 'ending' of the exposition. Indeed, it may seem overly reductive to speak of more than half of the exposition as its end. Rather, we more typically think of that end occurring much later in the game, perhaps at the final cadence of the group or even at the last codetta of the closing section. Consider, for example, the case where a single cadence is taken as the primary mechanism to end an exposition.[11] I would argue that such a cadence, say the one concluding the third subordinate theme (see the arrow in Figure 1.4), does not carry the entire burden of effecting expositional closure. Rather, this cadence can be understood as marking the 'end' of the theme, which marks the 'end' of the group, which marks the 'end' of the exposition. Given the hierarchical alignment of ending functions associated with this cadential unit, it is no wonder that many listeners may experience it as the 'real' end of the exposition.[12] Yet I would hold that, already at the beginning of the subordinate-theme group, we have entered into the temporal territory of expositional ending. Within this broad expanse of time, we can experience at lower levels of motion various articulations of beginning, being-in-the-middle, and ending. Eventually this large-scale ending function of the subordinate-theme group is fully completed—brought to its own end—by the final

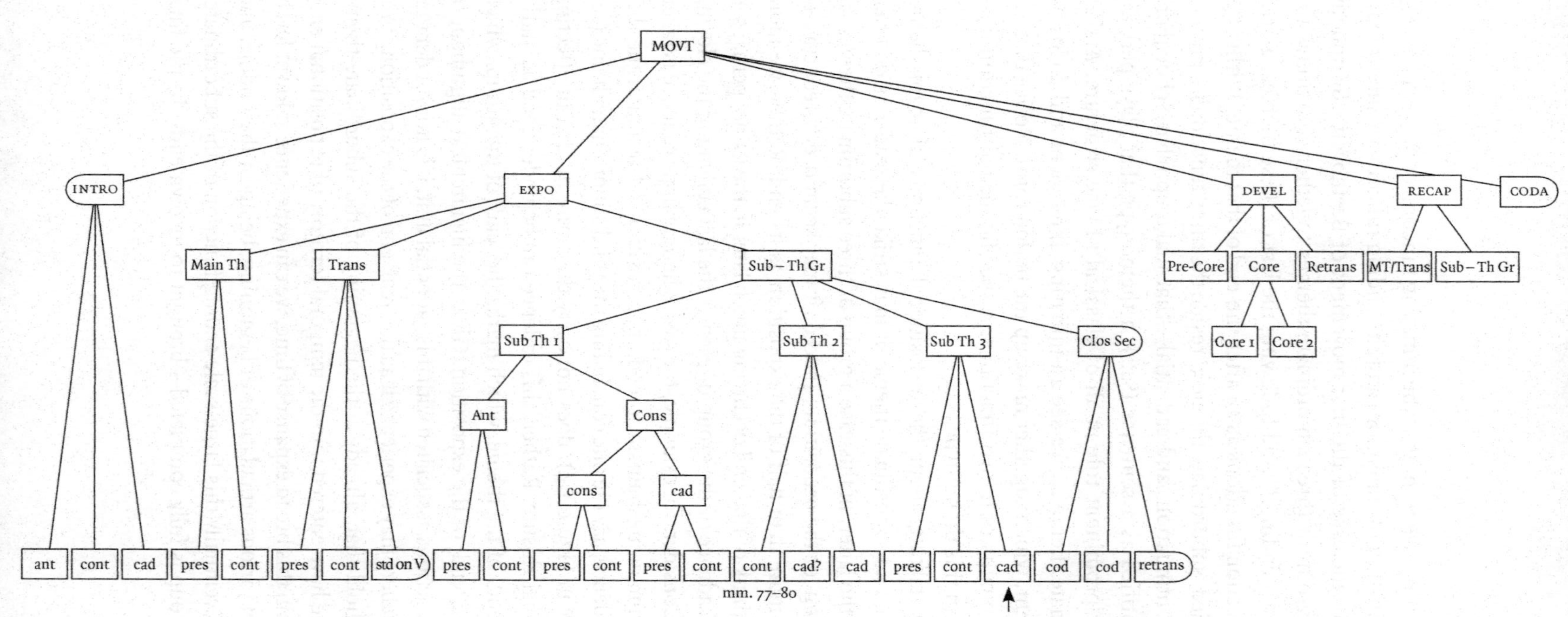

Figure 1.4 Ludwig van Beethoven, Symphony No. 1, Op. 21, i: formal functions

cadence, and what follows is a temporal after-the-end, taking the form of codettas. In short, the expression of formal ending arising at higher levels in the structural hierarchy of a work can span an enormous length of time, one that is similar to, or even at times exceeding, the time-spans associated with the processes of beginning and middle.

At this point we might ask how the traditional notion of 'closing theme' would fit into the form-functional view that I have been developing here. At least three options come to mind. In the first place, since almost all expositions bring a series of codettas following the final cadence of the subordinate theme (or theme group), such a collection of ideas, the very last to appear in the exposition, could be thought of as closing, even if the actual form-functional expression of these ideas is one of after-the-end. This is the option that I have adopted.[13] Since this group of codettas does not coalesce into a genuine theme (in particular, it does not bring any further cadential closure), I prefer the term 'closing *section*' to 'closing *theme*.'

If we want, however, to hold on to the notion of a specific 'closing *theme*,' then a second option would be simply to apply that label to the last subordinate theme of an exposition. In the case of Beethoven's First, the unit that I have identified as the third subordinate theme would then be considered the closing theme. As long as such a theme is understood to be equivalent to 'the final subordinate theme,' I would have no concerns. Such a usage allows us to retain the traditional idea of closing theme, though this term would not gain any additional functional meaning beyond that conveyed by 'subordinate theme.'

But if we go one step further and propose to identify a categorical distinction between subordinate theme on the one hand and closing theme on the other—and this would be option three—we enter into what I consider to be more problematic theoretical territory. For in all of my study of classical expositions, I have been unable to discover any clear and consistent compositional techniques that would permit one to posit such a functional differentiation. Thus a theme labeled as subordinate may employ the same phrase-structural procedures as found in a different theme, one considered closing. For example, an expanded cadential progression may be used to create a cadential arrival of powerful rhetorical strength for the first of several themes in the new key, but the same technique may be used instead to end the final theme of a group. In our Beethoven symphony, both the first and third themes in the new key conclude with expanded cadential progressions lasting nine bars (mm. 69–77, 92–100), though each is organized somewhat differently. The presence of an expanded cadential progression—a hallmark of expositions in the classical style—fails as a criterion for distinguishing between a subordinate theme proper and a putative closing theme. In fact, none of the devices used to characterize subordinate themes (as distinct, say, from main themes) can be seen as applying more typically to either the first or last theme in the new key.[14]

I recognize that it is hard to break away from some historically entrenched theoretical positions, but in the case of 'closing theme,' I find little advantage in holding on to this particular nomenclature and actually see a potential for form-functional confusion when trying to distinguish thematic units as subordinate or closing. In fact, the question of whether or not a specific closing theme should be included within the basic model of the classical sonata-form exposition may never find clear consensus. As Joel Galand notes, "[t]he conflict between Caplin and, say, Rothstein, over the boundaries of the closing section, though perfectly comprehensible, may be unresolvable for the simple reason that 'closing' is ultimately a rhetorical category that defies formal precision."[15] Still, until a theoretically consistent way of distinguishing closing theme from subordinate theme is firmly established, I find it preferable to identify *multiple* subordinate themes within many sonata expositions and to recognize the final group of codettas as the most useful unit to consider as 'closing.'

In the course of identifying some of the formal functions associated with the Beethoven Symphony, I made reference to 'sonata,' 'sentence,' and 'period.' These terms appear nowhere in Figure 1.4, however, and for good reason. For they do not in themselves refer to formal 'functions'; rather they stand for specific formal 'types.' This crucial distinction between function and type is highlighted in Table 1.1, which lists some representative full-movement types along with some theme types and associates each of them to a set of formal functions. This chart is not meant to be comprehensive, and I will not be discussing many of these items in any more detail. Rather, I want to emphasize that there are at least four good reasons for a theory of form to focus more on function than on type.

In the first place, the standard formal types traditionally identified by historians and theorists have not accounted for all of the syntactical arrangements of functions that arise in the repertoire. Thus, the possibility of mixing functions conventionally belonging to one type with those of another gives rise to 'hybrid' forms. In the case of theme types, I have identified at least four hybrids, the most common of which (shown at the bottom of Table 1.1) combines the antecedent of the period with the continuation and cadential functions of the sentence.[16]

A second advantage of attending more to function than type becomes evident when the set of functions of a given type remains incomplete. Consider mm. 77–80 from Beethoven's First (Example 1.1). Though these bars appear to 'begin' the second subordinate theme, they actually sound more medial in function, for they feature continuational characteristics such as sequential harmonies and repeated one-bar units. What follows in mm. 81–83 brings cadential harmonies, but in the wrong key. The theme finally ends with a genuine cadential function in mm. 84–88, culminating in a perfect authentic cadence. Thus while this theme contains two of the three functions of the sentence form—continuation and cadential—a clear functional beginning is actually missing, and so the theme seems to start, in some sense, already in its middle. By fixing our attention on this theme's constituent functions, we can be very precise on just how this particular sentence-like structure deviates from the norms of its type.

Thirdly, distinguishing between function and type permits us to attend to the fundamental building blocks of classical form without getting bogged down in unproductive debates about whether or not a given theme or movement represents a specific type. In my teaching experience, I have witnessed all too often students becoming fixated on trying to classify themes as sentences or periods, as if simply applying those labels were the central task at hand. Instead, I want them to focus on the constituent functions associated with these types and, for a particular theme, to answer more specific questions, such as, "Is the initiating phrase a presentation, an antecedent, or some combination thereof?" and "What kinds of cadential articulations are present in the theme?" Once we decide on its functional makeup, we can state with more confidence that the theme is a period or a sentence, or, even more typically, that it displays aspects of both types, either in the sense of a conventional hybrid or as some unique, non-conventional form.

At higher levels, the privileging of function over type distinguishes my approach from that of, say, Charles Rosen, or James Hepokoski and Warren Darcy, who identify a variety of 'sonata-form' types (emphasis on the plural) within the classical repertory.[17] I prefer instead to recognize a wider range of distinct, individual full-movement forms.[18] But more importantly—and this is the key point—I see classical form arising out of a common set of formal functions, which are deployed in different ways to create multiple full-movement types. The common element is not sonata form per se, but rather the functions that make up the various forms. Thus we can recognize the appearance of subordinate-theme function, to take one example, in a short minuet form, in a moderately-sized rondo form, in a large-scale concerto form, and, of course, in a sonata form. In each of these formal types, the notion of subordinate-theme function remains essentially the same, and the fundamental compositional techniques that define this function are manifest in similar ways throughout these differing forms.

A final reason to emphasize function over type is that in so doing, we more actively engage ourselves with musical time. As I have been stressing throughout, the various 'formal' functions are all manifestations of general 'temporal' functions. But the formal 'types' have no such determinate temporal expression. For example, a sentence form per se does not situate itself in any particular location in time. Only when a given sentence is identified functionally as, say, a main theme, does it attain the temporal status of a beginning. But a sentence may also be used as a subordinate theme, in which case it may be realized as an expositional ending. Formal types are thus atemporal, whereas the functions making up those types are intimately associated with our experience of time in music. A theory of form whose analytical methodology focuses primar-

Formal Types	Formal Functions
Full-Movement Types	
Sonata	Introduction Exposition main theme transition subordinate theme closing section Development Recapitulation Coda
Five-Part Rondo	Main Theme Subordinate-Theme Complex Main Theme Interior Theme Main Theme Coda
Large Ternary	Main Theme Interior Theme Main Theme
Concerto	Opening Ritornello Exposition Subordinate-Theme Ritornello Development Recapitulation Closing Ritornello
Theme Types	
Sentence	presentation continuation cadential
Period	antecedent consequent
Small Ternary	exposition (A) contrasting middle (B) recapitulation (A')
Hybrid Theme	antecedent [from period] continuation [from sentence] cadential [from sentence]

Table 1.1 Formal 'types' versus formal 'functions'

Example 1.1 Ludwig van Beethoven, Symphony No. 1, Op. 21, i, mm. 77–90

ily on details of formal functionality forces us to confront directly the processes that create musical time.

Let me now, in the final portion of this essay, briefly review the criteria used to identify formal functions. Here we must distinguish among hierarchical levels, for the criteria change depending upon whether the formal unit in question resides near the foreground or else embraces a larger stretch of time. At lower levels, the primary criterion is the kind of harmonic progression supporting the passage, in particular, whether the harmony is prolongational, sequential, or cadential.[19] In general, prolongational progressions engender a sense of formal initiation, sequential ones express medial functions, and cadential progressions create formal closure. Working closely together with harmony are important processes of grouping structure, especially that of fragmentation, in which units become increasingly smaller in relation to prior sounding units. Such fragmentation is highly expressive of medial functionality, especially in the case of the continuation function of the sentence.

But an opposite process—for which there is no standard term—can have important form-functional consequences as well. I am referring here to situations where larger-sized units are re-established following fragmentation. In some of those cases, the resumption of a larger unit can help to signal formal initiation. A good example occurs in the finale of Beethoven's *Pastoral* Symphony (Example 1.2). The passage shows the transition section of this rondo exposition beginning with a two-bar basic idea in the lower voices, which is repeated in the upper voices. The entire four bars are then restated with light ornamentation. The subsequent fragmentation and modulation to the new key render mm. 40–41 highly continuational, and the arrival at m. 42 on I^6 suggests potential cadential closure to end the transition. But instead of bringing an expected half cadence, the music sees a broadening of the grouping structure, and a new two-bar idea, one that prolongs the tonic of the new key, is established in mm. 42–43. A repetition of that idea, supported by dominant harmony, completes a presentation function. These bars are themselves repeated, thus establishing the four-bar unit as the large-scale group initiating a new thematic process. At m. 50, fragmentation into two-bar groups signals a medial, continuation function, and a subsequent cadential unit, beginning at m. 54, promises to bring closure to this new theme. In that it resides entirely in the key of the dominant, this is a fully legitimate subordinate theme, whose constituent initial, medial, and concluding functions are clearly articulated.[20] Even though the transition failed to bring its own cadential closure or any textural caesura, it is not difficult to hear the beginning of this subordinate theme, as signaled by the harmony and, especially in this case, by the grouping structure.[21]

Turning now from the lower-level phrase functions to the differentiation of higher-level thematic functions, the essential criterion is one of tonality, as confirmed by cadential articulation. Thus within an exposition, main-theme function concludes with a home-key cadence of some kind, either half or authentic; transition function destabilizes that key, usually by modulating to a new key; and subordinate-theme

Example 1.2 Ludwig van Beethoven, Symphony No. 6 (*Pastoral*), Op. 68, i, mm. 31–59

function requires authentic cadential confirmation of that new key. But tonality does not provide the whole story. For these thematic functions are also distinguished by a host of compositional processes that Schoenberg generalized under the notion of 'tight-knit' (*fest*) versus 'loose' (*locker*) formal organization. Figure 1.5 summarizes many of the factors that contribute to this fundamental distinction.[22] On this basis, we can observe that main-theme function normally defines the most tight-knit unit within a movement, against which can be measured the various other thematic functions as more or less loose. In particular, both transition and subordinate-theme functions are markedly looser than the main theme, though different loosening devices tend to be used within these functions respectively.

Now, I must admit a certain disappointment that the concept of tight-knit versus loose has yet to be as influential on current analytical practice as I believe is warranted. Thus whereas my categories for phrase functions have been widely adopted for analyzing tight-knit main themes, analysts have been slower to recognize that these same functions are also employed, albeit in a looser manner, in other formal regions. Perhaps the pedagogical tendency to teach phrase functions exclusively in connection with main theme types explains this lack of awareness. For when turning attention to larger formal concerns—such as transitions, subordinate themes, and development sections—students are rarely asked to account for the phrase-structural makeup of those broader units. But as soon as one attempts a detailed analysis of these functions, then a consideration of the various loosening devices comes readily to the fore, and the utility of conceptualizing, indeed truly experiencing, the varying degrees of tight-knit and loose organization proves invaluable.

So far, I have outlined the broad criteria used for identifying formal functionality. I want now to mention a criterion that plays a minimal role, namely, thematic content, or what I prefer to call 'melodic-motivic material.' Appeals to melodic content are typically grounded in two postulates. The first holds that the appearance of new ideas signals formal initiation. The second asserts that the return of a previously sounding idea brings its previously associated formal function. It is easy to understand why these postulates have proven irresistible to theorists. For the

	Tight-knit	→		Loose
tonality	home key (I)	subordinate key (V)	distant keys (iii, ♭VI)	modulating
harmony	prolongation of I	prolongation of I^6	prolongation of V	sequential
	diatonic		modal mixture	chromatic
cadence	PAC	HC	cadential evasion	no cadence
grouping structure	symmetrical (4 + 4)	(6 + 6)		asymmetrical (4 + 3 + 5)
motivic material	uniformity			diversity
thematic conventionality	period	sentence		non-conventional types

Figure 1.5 'Tight-knit' versus 'loose'

start of a new formal unit often brings new melodic-motivic ideas, and the return of prior materials regularly restores the formal context of the earlier appearance of those ideas. But frequency of occurrence can be deceptive, for it suggests a causal relation between content and function that, in my opinion, is erroneous.

Consider the *Pastoral* Symphony passage previously examined in Example 1.2. First, we can observe that m. 50 brings entirely new melodic-motivic material; but, as already discussed, this material is associated with a strong sense of being-in-the-middle of the subordinate theme. Second, we can note that mm. 42–45, which we identified as the beginning of that theme, brings no significant melodic change; in fact, the head motive, marked x, has been sounding throughout the prior transition. Finally, and now I am referring to the second postulate, the music at m. 54 brings back the rhythmic motives and melodic contour of the main theme's basic idea. But it would be wrong to speak here of a return to an initiating function; rather, this passage plays a decidedly cadential role.

In short, none of the standard associations between content and function are realized in this theme. Yet for this reason, identifying formal functionality should not be thrown into doubt; for the harmonic organization and grouping structure confirmed our functional interpretations without any consideration of the melodic-motivic materials. Indeed, such an appeal is rarely necessary even in passages where the association of content and function is more standard. That thematic content remains essentially independent of formal functionality turns out, in fact, to be an aesthetic boon. For the composer not only can forge an extensive web of motivic referentiality without disturbing the standard course of formal syntax, but can also cast new meanings to familiar ideas by allowing them to serve multiple functions. The listener in fact gains added pleasure from following the play between content and function, a game that can best be enjoyed when melodic-motivic ideas have no necessary connection to formal function.

Let me briefly conclude this essay by noting that more can be said about the nature of formal functions than I have had space here to pursue, including such topics as the potential for the 'retrospective reinterpretation' of formal functions or the 'fusion' of multiple functions within a single grouping unit. Though I have been stressing the important role of formal functionality, I want to assert, of course, that other aspects of musical organization participate in the broad concept of 'form in music,' and for this reason I can fully endorse a multivalent approach to formal analysis, such as that advocated by James Webster. As well, I acknowledge the important ways in which James Hepokoski, along with his collaborator Warren Darcy, have enriched our understanding of how dynamic and textural processes relate to the formal options available to composers. But no matter what approach a given analyst will favor, I am convinced that the value of understanding form in relation to musical time means that some account of formal functionality will certainly occupy a central place within any theory of classical form.

Comments on William E. Caplin's Essay "What Are Formal Functions?"

James Hepokoski

While the practice of Sonata Theory resonates in some substantial ways with William E. Caplin's form-functional theory, there are also a number of foundational areas in which these approaches diverge markedly. Some of these conceptual divergences have far-reaching consequences, and in this reply it would misrepresent the issues to downplay them. No close reader of the form-functional method could fail to observe (and admire) its rigorous logic and the single-minded insistences that drive its analytical ramifications. Once its premises and definitions are accepted and placed beyond question, all else follows: the dominos fall, one by one. But from the Sonata-Theory perspective, this is where our problems and differences begin. We dispute several of these premises; we consider some of its definitions (such as those of cadence, transition, subordinate theme, and closing ideas) either flawed or overly restrictive and inflexible; we find many of its analyses detached from history and (dialogical) context; and we are occasionally obliged to conclude that its pursuit of a mechanistically consistent, systematic reasoning sometimes overrides a more nuanced, more musical response and crosses the line into what we, at least, experience as the counterintuitive.

How useful is it to place temporal (and other) 'functions' at the radiating center of an analytical system, trumping other factors of one's musical experience? It goes without saying that function—the "unique temporal character" of "each time-span at the surface of the piece"—is an important aspect of a composition [>25]. But as defined here (with implicit nods to an underdeveloped phenomenology),[1] it is so self-evident as to border on the trivial. All temporal structures of whatever length must *ipso facto* have 'beginnings,' 'middles,' and 'ends,' and it is hardly revelatory to be reminded that there arose certain standardized ways of articulating these spans and that, for instance, even the 'middles' and 'ends' also feature their own 'beginnings' and 'middles,' and so on, in what is potentially an infinite regress.

Such basic experiences of functions (including 'before the beginning' and 'after the end') are so unremarkable that they are taken for granted within Sonata Theory, where they are integrated into larger concepts that we find to be more productive in confronting the complexities of a piece of music in the classical style or beyond. The much-insisted-upon "crucial distinction between function and [formal] type" ([>30]; see also Caplin's Table 1.1 [>33]) turns out to be a distinction without a significant difference. The formal types, after all, are largely defined and recognizable by their effecting of temporally situated formal functions (many of which Caplin defines harmonically, coupled with observations about fragmentation, tight-knit or loose organization, and so on). This means that to identify a type, such as a period or a sonata exposition, is always already to declare on behalf of a concomitantly implied internal function or ordered array of functions (encountered phenomenologically in real time by the listener). Any exceptional or unusual internal features that complicate one's perceptions may easily be pointed out as just that: exceptional (or, as we might characterize extreme cases, 'deformational'). While Caplin seems to be cautioning his readers against a simplistic reification of the term 'type,' that fear is overblown. One can applaud his desire that "we more actively engage ourselves with musical time" (who could disagree?), but in the end, it is difficult to understand the need to insist that "formal types are (...) [necessarily?] atemporal, whereas the functions making up those types are intimately associated with our experience of time in music" [>32]. What one comes away with is only the suspicion of hearing a doctrinaire reaffirmation that nearly all aspects of music, at nearly all levels of analysis, are to be dissolved back into little more than elemental beginning-middle-end functions, replicated *seriatim*, one after another.

Overinflating this single though certainly relevant factor into the master key of classical analysis leads Caplin, step by logical step, into a number of questionable claims. What is one to make of any system that declares that 'thematic content,' a central topical feature of the dramatized classical style by any account and one of the foremost attributes that all listeners directly experience, "plays [only] a minimal role" when compared with ever-recurring strings of beginning-middle-end functionalities [>37]? The dramatic textural contrasts and intertextually shared thematic/topical signs that such content regularly provides as vivid, expressive hallmarks of the style are thus demoted to a status "essentially independent of formal functionality," with "no necessary connection to formal function" [>39]. Even while granting the wiggle-room offered here by the qualifier 'necessary,' this seems an astonishing subordination of common sense to a dubious *a priori* postulate—to which Webster's advocacy of a more nuanced multivalence, coming to terms with the interactive implications of a richer surface, furnishes a welcome corrective.

Caplin's procedural lockstep may be grounded in a false hope that a quasi-scientific precision might still be obtainable in the area of analytical interpretation. As a result he finds himself tangled in definitional struggles that some readers might find more needlessly disputatious than enlightening. Consider his 'closing-theme' qualms. Here he has predecided that any theme that others might consider as in some sense 'closing' (even when that limited sense has been carefully defined) should not "employ the same phrase-structural procedures" [>29] as one occupying subordinate-theme space. A closing theme, for instance, cannot be shaped as a sentence. But why not? Who has declared this to be true? The reasoning here, as so much else in Caplin, is circular, tautological, an exercise in *petitio principii*: decisionistically, he predefines subordinate-theme space in a way that excludes any possibility of a fully developed closing theme or set of themes, then insists that what others have claimed as those themes are not justifiable by "any clear and consistent compositional techniques" that he has been able to "discover," notwithstanding "all of my study of classical expositions" [>29].[2]

From our perspective, it is difficult not to suspect that Caplin's formal-space definitions are sometimes uncritically declared at the outset as unassailable postulates (some of them perhaps too eagerly adapted from mid-century, problematic others, such as Schoenberg and Ratz) rather than as suggested concepts inductively derived from a patient rethinking of all of the interpretive possibilities at hand concurrently with a flexible and musically intuitive examination of the multiple realizations actually present in the repertory. The issue of identifying a presumed 'subordinate theme' in m. 42 of the sonata-rondo finale of the *Pastoral* Symphony, for instance, depends entirely on such definitions.

Sonata Theory would not interpret that measure as the onset of any such theme. (Indeed, it would regard the attempt to demonstrate that it *is* one—via the criteria of the form-functional system—to be a demonstration of the opposite, that is, of why that system's logic can lead to unconvincing assertions.) Instead, and not uncommonly in terms of expositional options, m. 42 advances the ongoing, midstream flow of a 'continuous exposition' (one lacking a medial caesura).

This matter boils down to assumptions and definitions—a discussion that would require more space than is available here. In brief, though: more intuitively and more in line with what we believe to be conventional (and accurate) construals, Sonata Theory normally grants secondary theme status only to themes prepared by a recognizable medial caesura—themes launched in the new key with a sense of restarting a process that had been brought to a literal or implicit rhetorical pause or equivalent articulation only moments before.[3] Not all expositions need to feature a secondary theme: those without an MC (continuous expositions) do not, a different exposition-type known since the mid-1960s to musicological scholars (especially Haydn scholars).[4] My sense, however, is that Caplin starts with the unnecessary assumption that all expositions *must* have a subordinate theme, which he then reconfigures, not surprisingly (since thematic content is downplayed), as a subordinate-theme 'function.'[5] One of its leading functions is to produce a PAC in the new key, a function that is axiomatically denied to all (pre-S) transitions (for instance, TRs—not yet S-spaces—that Sonata Theory would regard as ending in third- or fourth-level medial-caesura defaults, V:PAC MC or I:PAC MC).[6] Hence, for Caplin, it seems that if there is a V:PAC or equivalent anywhere in the exposition (as there almost always is), there must be something preceding it that is to be designated as a subordinate theme. And this sets him off on the hunt for one—as in the *Pastoral* finale.

In this case, the appeal (within an ongoing stream of modules) is made to the newly manufactured principle that in "situations where larger-sized units are re-established following fragmentation," such a "resumption of a larger unit can help to signal formal initiation" [>35]. With the triggering function-term "initiation" now lodged in place, he can assess m. 42 to be "a fully legitimate subordinate theme" [>35]. It all follows logically—but not musically, at least not to my ear. Measure

42, rather, is a reinvigorated, broader 'energy-burst,' joyously celebrating the music's exuberant move to the dominant key within a process of still-unfolding, obviously similar modules, driving ahead continuously from m. 32. This enlargement of formal units is a not-uncommon procedure within continuous expositions or within any passage of broader *Fortspinnung* that re-ignites or re-inflates itself midstream in order to keep plunging forward (instead of dissolving only once and forever into shorter units). It is the familiar strategy of a forward-vectored renewal, a new, well-placed modular burst continuing to propel the music onward, an opening into the next stage of a continuing relay.

It is true that we sense an *en-route* 're-energizing' at m. 42 of the *Pastoral* finale and it is indeed the onset of what may be regarded as a new sentence-presentation. But there is no need to call it a conceptually separable subordinate theme, unless, again, one has predefined the expositional situation in such a way as to demand the presence of such a theme. If one does demand this, though, one is placed in the position of pointing out structurally subordinate themes that otherwise, as here, would not initially be heard as such by many experienced listeners. Too-strict definitions too rigidly carried out can lead to counterintuitive conclusions. When they do, it is advisable to rethink those definitions.

Comments on William E. Caplin's Essay "What Are Formal Functions?"

James Webster

William E. Caplin's essay further develops the careful and patient classifications that characterize his *Classical Form*. Many of the principles and methods expounded are illuminating. These include his analytical multivalence, his distinction between 'tight' and 'loose' construction, and his well-grounded skepticism regarding many familiar notions in formal analysis, particularly the so-called closing group and the supposedly foundational role of musical ideas (and of distinctions among different types of themes) in creating form. I shall take all this for granted, and focus instead on the underlying argument, in which certain issues of logic and aesthetics seem to me not satisfactorily resolved. (Caplin acknowledges that his essay is a first attempt to explore these issues.)

In my reading, Caplin's argument depends on two primary theses. (1) Formal functions—main theme, transition, subordinate theme (or theme-complex), etc.—are 'temporal'; they are "manifestations of (...) generalized temporal functions" [>25]; that is, beginning, middle, and end (as well as 'framing' events). In practice they are understood as multivalent; each function "arises from criteria involving multiple parameters, most importantly harmony, tonality, grouping, and cadence" [>25]. (2) In their temporality, formal functions are fundamentally different from formal types: "I see classical form arising out of a common set of formal functions, which are deployed in different ways to create multiple full-movement types (...). Formal types are (...) atemporal, whereas the functions making up those types are intimately associated with our experience of time in music" [>32]. I will critique each thesis in turn.

(1) Formal functions as 'manifestations' of generalized temporal functions

If formal functions arise as 'manifestations' of generalized temporal functions, it is the latter—beginning/middle/end—that are foundational. However, I believe that these phenomena, precisely because of their ubiquity in human life and art, are *too* general to serve this theory-building purpose.[1] The difficulties are manifest in Caplin's Figures 1.2–1.4, devoted to Beethoven's Symphony No. 1. The verbal description of mm. 77–80 (the beginning of the second theme within the second group, highlighted in Figure 1.3; cf. Example 1.1) as "the 'beginning,' of the 'middle,' of the 'end,' of the 'beginning'" [>25] borders on the unintentionally comic (unless it is an unacknowledged trope of John Cage's *Lecture on Nothing*). And the corollary that composers "realize in a convincing manner these kinds of temporal multiplicities," such that *on this basis* experienced listeners can "discern quickly just where a particular passage lies" [>25] is not only unproved, but unprovable. In real life, nobody discerns the 'location' of such a fragment out of context, solely from complex beginning/middle/end characteristics of the sort ascribed to Beethoven's four measures, still less from its position in a notional tree-diagram; rather, we do so on the basis of the informed experience of listening to the work as a whole, in context: we *know* that a new idea within the second group is being initiated. That is, context determines function as much as function creates context.

The inadequacy of the beginning/middle/end paradigm as the basis for formal functions is obvious from the notion that the entirety of a long and complex second group has the function of 'ending,' merely because it occurs last within an exposition and ordinarily includes the structural cadence in the dominant. On the contrary, the function and 'feel' of mm. 53ff. of the Beethoven Symphony are those of initiation; Caplin's appeal to their supposed multi-functionality ('the beginning of the end') doesn't address this problem. Similarly, on both small and large scales the various possible functions are distinguished primarily by these same three elementary possibilities: on the small scale by "the kind of harmonic progression (...) prolongational, sequential, or cadential" (i.e. beginning, medial, ending) [>34], and on the large scale by "tonality [and] cadential articulation (...) main-theme function concludes with a home-key cadence (...) transition function destabilizes

(...) subordinate-theme function requires authentic cadential confirmation of [the] new key" (again: beginning, medial, or ending) [35]. This is too limited a 'repertory' of the kinds of things that can happen in a complex musical work.

Even after the insertion of formal functions in Figure 1.4, and (later) a discussion of the context of mm. 77–80, a fundamental problem remains. As implied in Caplin's third paragraph and his examples, the beginning/middle/end paradigm encourages (if it does not indeed require) the procedure of 'segmentation.' However, a segmentation diagram is merely a 'dead' sequence of successive fragments, until and unless it is 'animated' by a complementary representation of the work 'in action' (most obviously, a Schenkerian voice-leading graph). In terms of the binaries discussed in my essay "*Formenlehre* in Theory and Practice," only when the latter is supplied has one accounted for '*Formung*' as well as '*Form*.'[2] Moreover, segmentation diagrams suffer from the felt need to label every cell with a single, specific designation; the formal analyst abhors a 'naked' cell no less than nature a vacuum.[3] Thus in Figure 1.4, the unqualified label 'continuation' for mm. 77–80 is problematical, despite Caplin's claim that these measures are 'medial' in character. For they introduce a new idea, *piano* and in the minor (the bass deriving from m. 53); the well-marked oboe phrase in B-flat is as much presentational as continuational (despite the sequential repetition in G minor). Harmonically as well, since this theme is a minor-mode 'purple-patch,' the local function of m. 77 is initiatory rather than medial.[4] (Of course, Caplin is correct that this passage is the 'middle,' and least stable, unit within the second group as a whole; for this reason I share his skepticism of the pertinence of the concept 'closing' (group or theme) for the third unit, mm. 88–101.)[5]

(2) Formal functions versus formal types

Caplin's second thesis is that formal functions are temporal, whereas formal types are atemporal. A corollary is that formal functions are foundational (causes), while formal types are results (effects): "(...) form[s] *arising out of* (...) formal functions, which (...) *create* (...) full-movement types (...)" [>32, my italics]. I cannot accept these premises. Both distinctions—temporal versus atemporal; cause and effect—are rigid binarisms which, at least as far as the repertories under consideration here are concerned, more or less automatically self-destruct.

(a) *Temporal versus atemporal.* This distinction is analogous to those between '*Formung*' and '*Form*,' prolongation and segmentation, and indeed all the process–versus–structure binaries discussed in my essay. It is desirable and indeed often necessary to account for both aspects of form with respect to a given movement or section taken as a whole. However, the premise that there are *two distinct classes of musical entities*, one of which (formal functions) is temporal but the other (formal types) atemporal, flies in the face of both logic and experience. Caplin's example is 'sentence form' (listed as a 'theme type' in Table 1.1 [>33]), which "does not situate itself in any particular location in time" [>32]. Only when a given sentence "is identified functionally as, say, a main theme does it attain the temporal status of a beginning" however [>32], it may also be a subordinate theme, and so forth. Well, of course; any small- or medium-scale entity may appear in any number of locations. In fact, however, even the sentence is Janus-faced: it is described here as a 'form,' but once it becomes a main theme, it attains "the *temporal* status of a beginning" [>32, my italics]. Indeed, 'main-theme function' itself (like the others) is defined in terms of *both* location (beginning—although this borders on circular logic) *and* character (tight, prolongational, cadential, etc.). Similarly, in Table 1.1 'exposition' is listed as a formal function, and therefore typed as temporal (because it occurs 'at the beginning'). But an exposition as a whole self-evidently exhibits form as well; indeed Caplin himself applies his beginning/middle/end paradigm to expositions (see the indented entries in Table 1.1), which he thus understands as complete structures. Sentence, main-theme function, exposition: all three units unite aspects of temporality *and* structure, which in sophisticated tonal compositions cannot be dissociated.

(b) *Cause and effect.* Similarly, in artworks of this kind, any attempt to distinguish 'foundational' from 'secondary' aspects, or 'causes' from 'effects,' is doomed to failure. Caplin states that the formal types 'arise out of' the formal functions, but it is equally true that the functions arise out of the (pre-existing) need to create differentiation and progression within any given musical entity. In the compositional genesis of a theme, its basic motive or gestural character presumably often preceded any details of its working-out (such as whether it was to be a period or a sentence, or close on a half or full cadence, or even whether it was to be 'main' or 'subordinate'). And to the extent that the generalization holds that main themes are tight-knit, other themes looser, and transitions looser still, the decision that such-and-such an idea was to be (say) the main theme necessarily preceded the decision to work it out in a relatively tight manner.

A modest example of the dangers posed by an overly fixed linkage between type of theme and type of formal function can be seen in Caplin's analysis of a theme from the *Pastoral* Symphony (his Example 1.2 [>36]). I agree that the second theme begins *in medias res* on the I^6 chord in m. 42, and with a broadening: not of the grouping structure, however, which has been in 2s and 2+2s throughout, but of the harmonic rhythm, each chord now lasting two full bars: {(2+2)+(2+2)}. Hence to my ear mm. 50b–54a are not so much a 'fragmentation' (the two-bar grouping continues)[6] as an acceleration and enrichment of the harmony (faster harmonic rhythm; roots other than I and V); not so much a 'continuation' or a 'medial' function, as a new idea. Hence (even if at first counterintuitively) they are better understood as the closing theme, despite the extreme brevity of an 8+4-bar second group.[7] Indeed mm. 50b–54 (whether construed as 'closing' or not) bring the only PACs in C major; i.e. the structural cadence, whose status is confirmed by its recapitulation in the tonic, mm. 158–62.[8]

In short, I believe that all musical entities, on all levels, are temporal *and* structural: '*Form*' and '*Formung*.'

Response to the Comments

William E. Caplin

I thank my colleagues for their thoughtful and serious commentaries. Their remarks highlight crucial issues facing the contemporary *Formenlehre* and afford me the opportunity of clarifying and elaborating some of the positions that I staked out in my opening essay. In this response, I address what I take to be the major points of contention raised by my colleagues. These include the general goals of music theory, the specific goals of a theory of musical form, the experience of musical time, the relation of formal functionality to other aspects of form (formal type, thematic content, grouping structure), and the organization of sonata expositions (subordinate theme, closing theme). This response also permits me to raise some additional issues associated with my theory that I alluded to at the end of my opening essay (retrospective reinterpretation, form-functional fusion).

Included in the foregoing critiques are matters relating to the goals and methods of music theory in general. Thus James Hepokoski acknowledges that my theory is developed with "rigorous logic" [>41] and that its analytical applications are pursued with "single-minded insistences" [>41]. Yet he considers "some of its definitions (...) either flawed or overly restrictive and inflexible" [>41] and finds that "its pursuit of a mechanistically consistent, systematic reasoning sometimes overrides a more nuanced, more musical response and crosses the line into what we, at least, experience as the counterintuitive" [>41]. He further speaks of a "procedural lockstep" that "may be grounded in a false hope that a quasi-scientific precision might still be obtainable in the area of analytical interpretation" and of "definitional struggles that some readers might find more needlessly disputatious than enlightening" [>43]. At times he considers my reasoning to be "circular, tautological, an exercise in *petitio principii*" [>43]. And he concludes that "[t]oo-strict definitions too rigidly carried out can lead to counterintuitive conclusions. When they do, it is advisable to rethink those definitions" [>45].

These are serious charges. Yet rather than defending against them (for ultimately, they will have to be validated, modified, or rejected by others than myself or my colleague), I would rather respond to what I see as underlying issues regarding the general nature of music theory. For what I sense in Hepokoski's remarks is a certain suspicion and reluctance to embrace the development of systematic assumptions, definitions, and concepts, along with the attempt to apply such theoretical formulations with logical rigor in the course of analytical work.[1] He speaks of rigidities, inflexibilities, and "quasi-scientific precision" [>43] with such negative connotations as to suggest that a theory of music that strives for these qualities should be condemned from the start. But surely these same values could be interpreted in a more positive light as essential goals of any theoretical enterprise.

Some of Hepokoski's concerns may pertain to a distinction between 'theory' and 'analysis.'[2] As I stated in the introduction to *Classical Form* (in an attempt to forestall precisely the kind of critique leveled by Hepokoski), my "theory establishes strict formal categories but applies them flexibly in analysis."[3] By 'flexibly,' I largely mean the use of multiple concepts—each one being rigorously defined—in cases where ambiguities of structure present themselves. I do not mean constantly changing and revising the definitions in light of the compositional complexities presented by the music. This being said, there are nevertheless significant heuristic advantages of applying rigorous concepts to their logical end, for such a pursuit often leads to new modes of hearing familiar passages. In Beethoven's *Pastoral* finale, for example, Hepokoski derides my establishment of "the unnecessary assumption that all expositions *must* have a subordinate theme" [>44], which thus sets me "off on the hunt" [>44] for such a theme, one that "would probably never have occurred as such to experienced listeners" [>45]. I would counter that such analytical hunts can pay off handsomely and that even experienced listeners can come to new ways of hearing.[4] To be sure, the 'catch' may at times prove unenlightening (and I have no objections to Hepokoski, or anyone else, being unconvinced in the particular instance of the *Pastoral*), but I reject the implication that such analytical quests are, in principle, futile. They have, in fact, been part and parcel of almost all music-theoretical work throughout the ages.

The irony in Hepokoski's rebuke is that aspects of his own theory could be characterized in ways similar to how he has chastized mine. For his and Warren Darcy's Sonata Theory also establishes a number of firmly held concepts, such as the idea that a sonata exposition contains a single 'essential expositional close' (EEC) and the notion that, "[i]f there is no MC [medial caesura], there is no S [secondary theme]."[5] Each of these is as dogmatic an assertion as to be found in music theory from any era. It so happens that I disagree with both notions for a host of reasons, but I do not object, in principle, to their being proposed. In fact, such assumptions, postulates, definitions, and the like are a standard requirement of most theories.[6] In the end, the goals of a theory are to attain internal consistency, logic, and precision, and to produce analyses that are musically convincing and insightful. Whereas the value of the second goal is undisputed by all, it seems odd to criticize a theory for striving to achieve the first of these goals.

I turn now from the broad aims of any music theory to the more specific features of a theory of musical form and address the complaint, voiced by Hepokoski, that I place the concept of formal functions, especially as manifestations of more general temporal functions, "at the radiating center of an analytical system, trumping other factors of one's musical experience" [>41]. That I deem formal functionality to be central to my theory of form is undeniable; yet I reject the charge that formal functions override other modes of experiencing musical form. Figure 1.1 of my opening essay makes it clear that I see 'form' embracing a wide variety of organizing principles, only some of which directly relate to formal functions. No doubt motivic connections or various dynamic processes can impart to a musical work a particular 'shape' or 'form,' one which may be (but often is not) congruent with form-functional patterns. A theory of form has no need to suppress the shaping forces of any musical parameters, and a comprehensive account of musical form must take all such forces into consideration.

At the same time, when specific questions are asked about the hierarchical structuring of discrete musical events, then the act of identifying those events automatically brings forth a consideration of where they begin and end. And as soon as such temporal matters are broached, the issue of formal functionality emerges as a major concern. Though Hepokoski might feel that it is "hardly revelatory to be reminded that there arose certain standardized ways of articulating" time-spans that are characterized as a beginning, middle, or end [>41], I would counter that a main objective of any theory of form is precisely to account for those "standardized ways"; indeed, most all of my *Classical Form* is devoted to defining just which compositional techniques are responsible for generating formal functionality at all levels in a musical work. By placing functionality at the center of a formal theory, we are in a position to pose questions such as: "What are the conventional ways of structuring a main theme?"; "How is a transition different from a subordinate theme or a developmental core?"; "How are cadences created and how are they to be identified?". In fact, the analyses offered by my colleagues in their opening essays raise at every turn precisely these kinds of questions. I have no doubt that Hepokoski has indeed 'integrated' such concerns within his Sonata Theory, but to characterize the "basic experiences of functions" as "so unremarkable that they are taken for granted" [>42] is surely to underplay an essential aspect of musical form, one that has occupied a focal position in the history of *Formenlehre* from the mid-eighteenth century to the present.

Both of my colleagues express concerns about the phenomenology of musical time outlined in my opening essay. For Hepokoski, it is "underdeveloped" [>41], and for James Webster, the generalized temporal functions of beginning/middle/end (henceforth abbreviated B/M/E), "precisely because of their ubiquity in human life and art, are *too* general to serve" as foundational for the purpose of theory building [>47]. I concede that my model of musical time is rather primitive[7] and that these temporal functions represent, as Webster notes, "too limited a 'repertory' of the kinds of things that can happen in a complex musical work" [>48]. In trying to enrich my view, I thus proposed the notion of a hierarchical nesting of such functions, so that a given time-span on the musical foreground can be conceived to express multiple temporalities—seemingly at the same time, but really at different 'time-spaces,' to speak with Lewin.[8] And though my characterization of a passage from Beethoven's First as "the 'beginning,' of the 'middle,' of the 'end,' of the 'beginning'" was intentionally tongue-in-cheek [>25; quoted by Webster on >47], I did so in order to try to capture what we can perceive as temporally unique about that particular passage.[9] Webster, however, remains unconvinced, and in casting doubt on my notion that a subordinate theme group "ends" an overall exposition, he notes that "the function and 'feel' of mm. 53ff. (...) are those of initiation," and that my "appeal to their supposed multifunctionality ('the beginning of the end') doesn't address this problem" [>47]. I agree with him that these measures are entirely initiating at the level of the theme, but I also believe that a hierarchical approach to functionality can help us understand the particular location of these measures within the broader formal plan. For it is interesting to ask, could these measures (transposed into the home key) have been used to initiate the main theme? I suspect that few listeners would be satisfied with such an opening to the exposition.[10] In other words, something in the musical content of mm. 53ff. makes them entirely appropriate as the 'beginning' of the 'first' of three subordinate themes. Considerably more theoretical work needs to be directed toward understanding just which musical features help to project these kinds of multi-functionalities (as Webster puts it), but it is likely that rhythmical patterning, dynamics, and texture may play a significant role.[11]

Another issue in the phenomenology of time raised by Webster concerns my contention that experienced listeners "are able to discern quickly just where a particular passage lies within the overall temporal extent of a work" [>25]. I perhaps overstated the case here, but I suspect that some of my readers have had similar experiences to mine, where I will turn on the radio and be able to identify in a matter of seconds approximately where in the movement the music is located (e.g., toward the end of an exposition, in the middle of the development, at the start of a transition). Webster not only questions whether listeners can hear such formal functionality 'out of context,' but also suggests that the claim is "not only unproved, but unprovable" [>47]. Perhaps so, but some recent cognitive research conducted at McGill University supports the proposition that musically trained listeners can identify with statistically significant accuracy whether short passages, drawn from early Mozart piano sonatas and heard in isolation, occur as the beginning, middle, or end of a thematic unit.[12] If this is so, then something in the musical materials themselves, irrespective of the listeners knowing the broader context, articulates a sense of temporal location. I am not proposing, of course, that context plays no role; it obviously contributes to our presuming the formal function of a passage. When we hear that something has ended, we well expect that what follows will be a new beginning. But until we hear that the musical content itself projects a clear sense of initiation, our interpretation remains somewhat provisional and open to subsequent reinterpretation of what temporal function is actually being expressed.

Webster's critique of my hearing as 'continuational' the very start of the second subordinate theme (m. 77) of Beethoven's First Symphony relates directly to this question (see Example 1.1 [>34]). He counters that these measures are more rightly to be heard as initiating, "[f]or they introduce a new idea, *piano* and in the minor" [>48]. I agree that the opening I–IV progression projects a sense of beginning, especially in the context of an elided PAC closing the first subordinate theme. But when the progression continues on to realize a broader sequential pattern, it is possible to *reinterpret* the formal situation and understand that medial functionality is already being expressed from the very start of the theme; in other words, a more traditional initiation (in which an opening I–IV statement would be completed as a tonic prolongation by a V–I response) has been bypassed altogether. Webster is correct to ask that we be careful in our labeling, and perhaps the notion of 'initiation *becomes* continuation' more fully captures the subtleties of this passage rather than exclusively choosing either one of these functions as the main descriptor.

I turn now to how formal functionality relates to formal types, thematic content, and grouping structure.

(1) *function versus type.* With respect to the distinction that I draw between formal functions and formal types, both colleagues object to my suggesting that the former are linked to temporal functionality while the latter are not. When speaking of types (such as sonatas, rondos, ternaries, periods, hybrids) as atemporal, I do not mean that a given exemplar of a type does not unfold in time or that it does not express a sense of beginning, middle, or end. What I mean is that, *as an abstract category*, a formal type has no predetermined relation to a temporal function. Therefore, when exploring the temporality of a particular type, one needs to identify the specific case (e.g., a sentence), study its internal functions (e.g., presentation, continuation, and cadential), and then consider the broader function that the type serves as whole (e.g., as first subordinate theme). My "fear," which I do not believe is "overblown" (as Hepokoski puts it [>42]), is that focusing on type over function lets the analyst too quickly off the hook of providing a detailed functional justification for the labeling of any given type. In the end, I am not claiming enormous significance for this distinction, but I do find it to be of considerable heuristic value in the ways that I describe in my opening essay.

(2) *function versus thematic content.* My assertion that "thematic content remains essentially independent of formal functionality" [>39] leads Hepokoski to charge that, in "an astonishing subordination of common sense to a dubious *a priori* postulate" [>43], my system "declares that 'thematic content' (...), one of the foremost attributes that all listeners directly experience, 'plays [only] a minimal role' when compared with ever-recurring strings of beginning-middle-end functionalities" [>42]. Here, I believe that my colleague has misunderstood the intent of my claim. For I am manifestly not saying that thematic content plays a minimal role in our experience of music; in fact, it clearly plays a major role (perhaps for most listeners, *the* major role). What I am claiming is that thematic content does not contribute essentially to how the functionalities of B/M/E come into being. This point is not meant to undermine the significance of thematic content in general, but rather its significance as a factor in making analytical decisions about where formal units begin or end. It is fair enough

to take issue with this assertion, and I would welcome continued debate on the matter; but then we should expect detailed demonstrations showing how thematic content—independent of harmonic and grouping-structural aspects—determines formal functionality.

(3) *function versus group*. Webster correctly observes that the B/M/E paradigm "encourages (...) the procedure of 'segmentation'" [>48] or what I call *grouping* analysis. He raises concerns, however, that "a segmentation diagram is merely a 'dead' sequence of successive fragments, until and unless it is 'animated' by a complementary representation of the work 'in action' (most obviously, a Schenkerian voice-leading graph)" [>48]. Webster's point is well taken: most tree diagrams suffer by appearing abstract and static, and compared with a Schenkerian representation, which by its very nature is more 'musical,' they may seem lifeless and empty of real content. Moreover, such analyses tend to project a certain rigidity in order to respect principles of hierarchical 'well-formedness.'[13] Thus a grouping analysis cannot easily account for structural overlaps, for the explicit relationships of groups that are non-consecutive (at a given level), or for retrospective reinterpretations. But whereas these limitations apply especially to an uninterpreted grouping analysis (of the kind shown in Figure 1.2 of my opening essay [>24]), the further step of specifying the formal function of the groups, such as that in Figure 1.4 [>28], permits greater analytical flexibility than Webster seems to appreciate. For although a single group typically serves a single function, the relation between these two is often more complex. Two common situations involve (1) the possibility that a formal function may embrace multiple groups, such as when a highly expanded cadential function ending a subordinate theme consists of multiple phrases, and (2) when one group embraces two or more functions, a situation that I term 'fusion.' As well, a given group might initially be understood to project one function, but then come to be reinterpreted retrospectively as another one. In short, grouping and function are often congruent, but sometimes not; that they arise from different musical relationships means that while they may interact in significant ways, they represent essentially distinct aspects of musical form.

To conclude, let me respond to some concerns raised by my notions of sonata exposition, especially the nature and status of subordinate and closing themes. Hepokoski takes me to task for rejecting 'closing theme' as a category of form. He believes that I have "predecided that any theme that others might consider as in some sense 'closing' (...) should not 'employ the same phrase-structural procedures' as one occupying subordinate-theme space. A closing theme, for instance, cannot be shaped as a sentence. But why not? Who has declared this to be true?" [>43]. I respectfully submit that my colleague has misconstrued the point of my critique. For I am not asserting that the phrase structure of a closing theme must differ from that of a subordinate theme (and I never claimed it could not be a sentence). What I am asking for is a clear definition of what would functionally differentiate such themes, and I suggested that locating a distinction in terms of phrase structure would be an obvious place to look. Failing that, however, I would be happy to recognize a category of closing theme if we could discover any other means of defining its properties, for example, that it is generally louder than a subordinate theme, or longer, or texturally more complex, or that it brings some characteristic melodic formations. Unfortunately, I have yet to uncover any such distinguishing properties. And when considering what prior theorists have labeled as a closing theme, I find no consistent criteria used to make that identification, other than the analytically trivial one that it appears *last* in the exposition. Thus my rejection of closing theme as a functional category is not made out of any 'predecision' or any perverse desire to buck theoretical tradition. Rather, I have been led to this viewpoint by carefully considering how such a thematic category could be meaningfully developed and analytically employed, and I have concluded—for the time being at least—that it is entirely dispensable, that the concept of *subordinate theme* adequately covers the formal situations presented in the later portion of a sonata exposition.[14]

As for my understanding of subordinate theme and my specific analysis of that function within Beethoven's *Pastoral* finale, Hepokoski correctly locates the source of our disagreements at the level of fundamental "assumptions and definitions" [>44]. Space limitations prohibit an extended discussion of how our concepts differ, but a number of points are worthy of mention nonetheless. Sonata Theory "normally grants secondary theme status only to themes prepared by a recognizable medial caesura" [>44]. In the absence of such a caesura, the theory proposes to view the exposition as 'continuous' and thus lacking any subordinate theme. Now this is a curious idea: for whether or not a stretch of music in the new key is regarded as a subordinate theme seems to depend more on what *precedes* the passage in question, rather than on its actual content.[15] But is this how we really experience music? To be sure, our initial understanding of a passage may well be influenced by how it is set up. But eventually we hear what the passage itself is telling us about its formal expression. The effect of a medial caesura may provide an appropriate *textural* backdrop for the beginning of a new theme, but ultimately the sense of initiation must be articulated by the nature of the musical materials found there. Moreover, the absence of a medial caesura should not preclude hearing thematic initiation based on the cues that the music actually offers (such as the establishment of a basic idea supported by a tonic prolongation or by the reconsolidation of the grouping structure into broader units, a criterion that I introduced in my opening essay).

Inasmuch as the exposition of the *Pastoral* finale contains no medial caesura, Hepokoski identifies a continuous exposition there and thus, logically in terms of Sonata Theory, no subordinate theme. He therefore explains the expansion of the grouping structure at m. 42 (which for me, helped to project the beginning of the subordinate theme) as "a reinvigorated, broader 'energy-burst,' joyously celebrating the music's exuberant move to the dominant key" [>45], and he further notes that such "enlargement of formal units is a not-uncommon procedure within continuous expositions or within any passage of broader *Fortspinnung* that reignites or reinflates itself midstream in order to keep plunging forward" [>45]. Hepokoski's description is accurate and evocative; it also complements well my own account. He even concedes that the "'re-energizing' at m. 42 (...) is indeed the onset of what may be regarded as a new sentence-presentation" [>45], that is, a structural initiation. But he then asserts that even so, "there is no need to call it a conceptually separable subordinate theme" [>45].

Of course, Hepokoski must deny the existence of a subordinate theme in the *Pastoral* finale according to the demands of Sonata Theory, which posits a fundamental distinction between a 'two-part exposition' (containing medial caesura and subordinate theme) and a continuous one (containing neither). But, in fact, there are good reasons to identify a subordinate theme there. For in so doing, we not only account for many details of the formal organization, but we also identify a continuity of compositional practice informing both two-part and continuous expositions. If it can be demonstrated—and I believe it can—that continuous expositions bring either a complete subordinate theme or sufficient functional elements of such a theme (one that 'fuses' with the prior transition),[16] we can recognize that all expositions employ the same basic formal syntax. Separating them as two-part or continuous, while useful enough in relation to textural, rhythmic, and dynamic processes, obscures the underlying logic of formal functionality adopted by the classical composers.

Indeed, distinguishing between the 'syntax' and 'rhetoric' of musical form might point the way to an eventual reconciliation of some fundamental conflicts between a theory of formal functions and Sonata Theory.[17] For whereas the former deals largely with the syntactical succession of formal units by rigorously focusing on harmonic progression and grouping structure, the latter brilliantly exposes the rhetorical, expressive, and hermeneutic effects of such units by carefully attending to texture, dynamics, instrumentation, and the like. By combining aspects of both theories (and thus emphasizing a multiplicity of parameters, as called for by Webster in Part III of this volume), we can provide a richer view of classical form than by employing either theory alone. Toward the goals of highlighting differences in approach as well as of resolving points of divergence, it is to be hoped that the 'multivalent dialogues' initiated in the present collection of essays will continue to be pursued—not only by myself and my colleagues—but by the many theorists and historians who find the theory of form a continual source of intellectual fascination and musical reward.

Notes

WHAT ARE FORMAL FUNCTIONS?

William E. Caplin

1. William E. Caplin, *Classical Form: A Theory of Formal Functions for the Instrumental Music of Haydn, Mozart, and Beethoven* (1998). Support for the research reflected in that book as well as in the essays of the present volume was provided by the Social Sciences and Humanities Research Council of Canada.

2. In the glossary, I eventually defined 'formal function' as follows: "The specific role played by a particular musical passage in the formal organization of a work. It generally expresses a temporal sense of beginning, middle, end, before-the-beginning, or after-the-end. More specifically, it can express a wide variety of formal characteristics and relationships" (*Classical Form*, pp. 254–55). The first and third sentences are overly general and not particularly helpful; the second sentence, though, does establish the fundamental relation between functionality and temporality that I develop more fully in the present essay.

3. To save space, I have omitted lower-level groupings for the later portions of the movement.

4. The most comprehensive and formalized theory of grouping structure is found in Fred Lerdahl & Ray Jackendoff, *A Generative Theory of Tonal Music* (1983), pp. 13–17, 36–67.

5. For the second level from the top, I have begun the lettering with the exposition section, not the slow introduction. This adjustment helps reveal the large-scale A–B–A' patterning associated with the fundamental sonata form lying at the basis of the movement.

6. V. Kofi Agawu, *Playing with Signs: A Semiotic Interpretation of Classic Music* (1991), Chapter 3.

7. The idea of a hierarchical multiplicity of temporalities is hardly confined to musical situations; rather, it can be seen to inform a human being's experience of time in a host of everyday contexts. To take one mundane example relevant here: I delivered the oral version of this essay as the third of three papers (ending), at the first portion (beginning), of a late-afternoon round-table (ending), on the third day (middle) of the Freiburg EuroMAC conference. These multiple expressions of temporal location combined together to imbue my presentation with a unique placement in the 'time' of the conference as a whole, a placement that had a palpable, psychological effect on my own experience of reading the paper.

8. Arnold Schoenberg, *Fundamentals of Musical Composition* (1967); Erwin Ratz, *Einführung in die musikalische Formenlehre: Über Formprinzipien in den Inventionen und Fugen J. S. Bachs und ihre Bedeutung für die Kompositionstechnik Beethovens* (1973). Schoenberg and Ratz largely confine their notion of formal functionality to relatively high levels in a movement's hierarchical structure. Thus Ratz's '*funktionelle Formenlehre*' has at its basis an *Urform* consisting of five parts: "(...) one part that exposes the tonic, a second part that leads away from the tonic (transition, first episode), a part that lingers in distant regions (subordinate

theme, development), a part that leads back to the dominant of the home key (retransition), and a part that reinforces the newly achieved tonic" (ibid., p. 56, my translation). A major goal of *Classical Form* is to provide functional interpretations for all levels in the formal organization of a movement.

9. I am using the term 'theme' not just in the sense of 'melody,' but rather as a complete middle-ground structural unit consisting of multiple phrases leading to cadential closure. Some theorists speak of this structure as a single 'phrase' (William Rothstein), a 'period' (Leonard Ratner), or even a 'paragraph' (James Webster).

10. For a more detailed analysis of the subordinate-theme group of this exposition, see William E. Caplin, "Structural Expansion in Beethoven's Symphonic Forms" (1991), pp. 33–36.

11. I discuss the idea that cadence can be viewed as an ending function for an entire exposition, along with the more general issue of the hierarchical limitation of cadential closure, in William E. Caplin, "The Classical Cadence: Conceptions and Misconceptions" (2004), pp. 60–66. The most prominent exponents of the position that a sonata exposition normally features a generically 'concluding' cadence are James Hepokoski and Warren Darcy, whose concept of 'essential expositional closure' (EEC) is based on the identification of a single cadence that is deemed to conclude an 'essential' exposition, even while much closing material may follow (including later cadences, which would 'end' the exposition in a different sense); see James Hepokoski & Warren Darcy, *Elements of Sonata Theory: Norms, Types, and Deformations in the Late-Eighteenth-Century Sonata* (2006).

12. The salience accruing to the moment of multiply hierarchical endings is similarly associated with the very moment of formal initiation; thus m. 13 of Beethoven's First Symphony is highly marked as the 'beginning' bar, of the 'beginning' phrase, of the 'beginning' theme, of the 'beginning' section, of the entire movement. By contrast, the alignment of medial functions would not seem to create any special moment of perceptual significance.

13. *Classical Form*, p. 122.

14. A major criterion used by Hepokoski and Darcy to distinguish the secondary-theme zone (S) from the closing zone (C) is 'melodic differentiation'—the statement of a 'new' (not-S-based) theme following the first satisfactory PAC in the subordinate key, their 'essential expositional closure' (EEC). (Restatements of all or part of S are considered as remaining in an expanded S-space.) Thus in the case of Beethoven's First Symphony, they note that one's initial assumption that the cadence at m. 77 will serve as the EEC, the moment that divides S from C, becomes undermined: "Instead of moving directly into C, S-material is retained with a sardonic, *pianissimo*, after-the-fact back-reference to the opening of S" (*Elements of Sonata Theory*, p. 125). The EEC proper, and thus the beginning of C, only appears at m. 88, where "characteristic S-melodic-material is (...) relinquished with a shift into differing ideas" (ibid., note 14). Later in this essay, I question whether melodic differentiation of this kind is a legitimate ground for distinguishing among formal functions. A different criterion for identifying closing themes is proposed by David Temperley, who suggests that closing themes tend to feature an end-accented grouping structure, as opposed

to subordinate themes, which are normally beginning-accented; see David Temperley, "End-Accented Phrases: An Analytical Exploration" (2003), pp. 132–36. Problematic in Temperley's account, however, is that most of the 'themes' that he identifies are actually groups of codettas that function as either genuine closing sections or make up the first part of a more complete thematic unit. Thus any proposed differentiation between subordinate theme and closing theme must also develop a consistent definition of 'theme' (see note 9, above).

15. Joel Galand, "*Formenlehre* Revived" (2001), pp. 192–93; the reference to William Rothstein involves that theorist's proposal that a closing theme can be identified as that portion of the exposition "following the first strongly articulated perfect cadence in the goal key"; see *Phrase Rhythm in Tonal Music* (1989), p. 116.

16. See *Classical Form*, Chapter 5, for a discussion of four hybrid theme types.

17. Rosen speaks of a 'minuet sonata form' and a 'finale sonata form' in addition to the standard 'first-movement sonata form'; see *Sonata Forms* (1988), Chapter 6. Hepokoski and Darcy identify five differing sonata-form types (*Elements of Sonata Theory*, pp. 344–45), the fifth of which embraces concerto first-movement form.

18. In *Classical Form*, I define, along with 'sonata form,' an overall 'minuet/trio form,' a more specific 'minuet form,' two main types of 'rondo form' (with some additional variants), 'concerto form,' 'sonata without development form,' 'large ternary form,' and 'theme and variations form.'

19. On my tripartite scheme for classifying harmonic progressions, see *Classical Form*, Chapter 2.

20. As it turns out, this subordinate theme lacks a concluding moment of cadence, a functional deviation that occurs now and then in rondo forms, where the need to dramatize, or even fully to confirm the subordinate key—essential to the aesthetic of sonata form—is downplayed in favor of emphasizing the return to the rondo refrain, usually through an extensive retransition; see *Classical Form*, p. 237. Some listeners may want to identify cadential articulations arising earlier within this theme; thus the resolution of dominant to tonic at m. 50 may prompt an interpretation of imperfect authentic cadence at this moment. But not only does the preceding passage lack a genuine cadential progression (the dominant functions throughout as a neighboring harmony within a tonic prolongation), but m. 50 cannot be understood to represent a formal 'end,' seeing as everything up to this point has been expressing an initiating presentation function. The tonic harmonies of mm. 52 and 54 might also strike the casual listener as points of potential cadence, but Beethoven is careful to invert the preceding dominants in order to prohibit the formation of genuine cadential progressions and to keep the harmonic context fluid, as is appropriate for the continuation function being expressed during these measures.

21. The criterion of an enlarged grouping structure helps to identify the beginning of the subordinate theme in a number of problematic cases from Beethoven's later piano sonatas; see Op. 78, i, m. 20; Op. 81a, i, m. 39; and Op. 110, i, m. 20. In all of these expositions, the transition lacks a concluding formal function such that the beginning of the subordinate theme is not immediately evident.

22. See *Classical Form*, pp. 84–86, for an elaboration in prose of Figure 1.5.

COMMENTS ON WILLIAM E. CAPLIN'S ESSAY "WHAT ARE FORMAL FUNCTIONS?"

James Hepokoski

1. Compare Caplin's light-touch treatment of the experience of temporality within a diachronically unfolding art with, e.g., that of Wolfgang Iser, *The Act of Reading: A Theory of Aesthetic Response* (1978), or, within the field of music theory, with the concerns of David Lewin in such writings as "Music Theory, Phenomenology, and Modes of Perception" (1986).

2. Claims of this sort lie at the heart of Caplin's objections to Sonata Theory's heuristic, historically informed concept of essential expositional and structural closure (EEC and ESC), along with our conceptions of secondary and closing themes, which we elaborated at length, in flexible and nuanced ways (including multiple exceptions and problematic cases), in my and Warren Darcy's *Elements of Sonata Theory* (2006). One cannot rehearse all of these EEC-arguments here.

3. *Elements of Sonata Theory*, Chapters 3 and 4, pp. 23–64. Some exceptions are noted on pp. 47–50. The normative guideline, however, is that "if there is no MC, there is no S. If there is no medial caesura, we are confronting not a two-part exposition but a continuous exposition, for which the concept of S is inappropriate" (p. 117).

4. Jens Peter Larsen, "Sonata Form Problems" (1988), pp. 269–79; Michelle Fillion, "Sonata Exposition Procedures in Haydn's Keyboard Sonatas" (1981). Charles Rosen also wrote of Haydn's occasional 'three-part organization' in *Sonata Forms*, pp. 100-04, and provided an example with the Symphony No. 44 (*Trauer*), first movement.

5. E.g., Caplin, *Classical Form*, p. 97: "In line with the fundamental precepts of this book, however, a subordinate theme refers not only to a thematic unit but also to a definite formal function," and "one of the theme's principal functions [is that of] confirming the subordinate key." In practice, I presume that the reverse is also true, namely, that a subordinate-theme function also refers to a concrete thematic unit that is selected to be designated as the subordinate theme. Caplin additionally refers to other functions of the 'constituent phrases' of S: "an *initiating* function of some kind (antecedent, presentation, or compound basic idea), a *medial* function (continuation), and a *concluding* function (cadential or, more rarely, consequent). Framing functions, such as introduction, codetta, and standing on the dominant are frequently associated with the theme as well" (p. 97). S themes are also more 'loosely organized' than P-themes, in a variety of ways described in several passages in the book.

6. *Elements of Sonata Theory*, pp. 27–29 brings up issues, problems, and examples of the V:PAC and I:HC MC. So far as I can tell (it may never actually be stated point-blank), Caplin, in *Classical Form*, grapples with this matter by assuming that any I:PAC immediately preceding a (new-key) S must actually mark the end of a P-function (and thus such an exposition would lack a transition, suggested though not illustrated, e.g., on p. 211) and that the V:PAC must already, by definition, be the result of a subordinate theme function (see note 5 above). Con-

sequently, when confronting expositions where a clearly marked 'subordinate theme' seems to be absent or problematic, Caplin—setting aside more intuitive alternatives—is obliged to devise such strained categories as 'obscured boundary between transition and secondary theme,' 'transition lacking a concluding function,' 'transition/subordinate-theme fusion,' and the like (pp. 135, 201–03).

COMMENTS ON WILLIAM E. CAPLIN'S ESSAY "WHAT ARE FORMAL FUNCTIONS?"

James Webster

1. Caplin appeals to Kofi Agawu's use of the beginning/middle/end paradigm as a foundational concept of 'introversive semiosis,' in *Playing with Signs* (1991), but Agawu's procedure suffers from the same problematic.

2. As is done, for example, by Lerdahl and Jackendoff (cited by Caplin), who rightly insist on the complementary roles of grouping structure (segmentation) and prolongational structure (dynamic form). Indeed Lerdahl's more recent *Tonal Pitch Space* (2001) explicitly assigns a higher status to prolongational structure.

3. An analogous danger attaches to topical analysis: often, every distinct motive is specified as instantiating some topic or other (as in Leonard G. Ratner's analysis of the introduction to the *Prague* Symphony, discussed in Agawu, pp. 17–20), whether or not all these topics are persuasive.

4. In my view the B-flat tonicization comprises only mm. 79–81, corresponding to the first oboe phrase; m. 82 (the second phrase) returns immediately to G minor.

5. As described in the reference in his note 11 [>63].

6. Measure 54a 'counts,' because of the cadential arrival on its downbeat (which, by elision, also functions as the beginning of the next idea).

7. But then part of its point is that everything is drastically compressed by comparison with the leisurely first group; this is not uncommon in sonata-rondos.

8. As Caplin notes, mm. 54–56 appear to launch a much stronger PAC, which however is subverted (again faithfully replicated in the recapitulation). However, he states incorrectly that mm. 51–52 and 53–54 are not genuinely cadential, because the dominants are in inversion. Perhaps he was misled by his piano reduction (cf. his Example 1.2 [>36]), in which the lowest notes represent the cellos; in the score and to the ear, however, these dominants are unambiguously long notes in root position, sounded by double-basses and second bassoon and doubled by the violas.

RESPONSE TO THE COMMENTS

William E. Caplin

1. To be clear, I am referring here specifically to the remarks in his commentary to my essay, not to his actual theorizing in Hepokoski & Darcy, *Elements*

of Sonata Theory. As I will mention shortly, this theoretical work can readily be characterized as systematic and comprehensive.

2. Though this distinction is not entirely hard and fast, I generally subscribe to David Lewin's characterization of their essential difference (See David Lewin, "Behind the Beyond: A Response to Edward T. Cone" (1969), pp. 59–69.

3. *Classical Form*, p. 4.

4. I am thus gratified that James Webster concurs in my finding a subordinate theme to begin at m. 42.

5. Hepokoski & Darcy, *Elements of Sonata Theory*, p. 117.

6. Indeed, my own approach has its own dogmas, such as the one (already observed by Hepokoski) that a sonata exposition requires the presence of subordinate-theme function. Another of my dogmas insists that dominant harmony appear in root position in order to speak of its projecting a cadential harmonic function.

7. And Webster graciously reminds the reader that my essay "is a first attempt to explore these issues" [>46].

8. David Lewin, "Music Theory, Phenomenology, and Modes of Perception" (1986), pp. 327–92.

9. The idea of nested functions is, of course, well known in Schenkerian theory, where a given harmonic entity, say, the final cadential event of an expositional subordinate theme, is understood as 'tonic' at one level of structure (within the theme itself) but as 'dominant' at a higher level (within the context of the movement as a whole). To take a more extreme case, consider the F^7 harmony in m. 79 of Beethoven's First (see Example 1.1 in my opening essay [>34]), which may be multiply described as the 'dominant seventh,' of the 'flat-mediant,' of the 'dominant,' of the 'tonic.'

10. Likewise, listeners would probably find it odd for a subordinate theme to begin with the materials of mm. 13ff.

11. As I noted in *Classical Form* (p. 197), "Many main themes exhibit a certain hesitancy or uncertainty in the course of their unfolding, often bringing sudden, striking changes in texture and marked discontinuities in rhythmic momentum." These features well describe what happens at mm. 13ff. of Beethoven's First. By contrast, subordinate themes tend to exhibit a greater uniformity of rhythm and texture; thus mm. 53ff. bring a continuous accompanimental patterning, and the rhythmical gaps in the oboe melody are filled in by the motivic imitations in the flute.

12. See Michel Vallières, Daphne Tan, William E. Caplin, Joseph Shenker, and Stephen McAdams, "Intrinsic Formal Functionality: Perception of Mozart's Materials" (2008). Non-musically trained listeners were far less accurate in making such functional identifications. Especially interesting were those cases where ambiguities of interpretation arose, particularly as regards beginnings vs. middles. Subsequent analysis of such passages permitted us to hypothesize which musical parameters were responsible for the functional uncertainties. Needless to say, further research will be needed to confirm these results and to test whether larger time-spans are similarly capable of being perceived as having an 'intrinsic' functional interpretation.

13. Fred Lerdahl & Ray Jackendoff, *A Generative Theory of Tonal Music* (1983), pp. 37–39.

14. As discussed in my opening essay, however, I do recognize a postcadential 'closing section' consisting of a group of codettas, which do not organize themselves into a full-fledged theme.

15. Something similar appears to be operative in the case of Sonata Theory's 'closing zone,' whereby its onset is primarily determined by the location of a *preceding* essential expositional close: "By definition C is postcadential (post-EEC). Normally we cannot consider anything to be C until S has attained the EEC" (*Elements of Sonata Theory*, p. 180).

16. See *Classical Form*, pp. 201–203.

17. For a more specific application of the distinction between syntax and rhetoric to the realm of cadence, see Caplin, "The Classical Cadence" (2004), pp. 106–12.

PART II
James Hepokoski

&

THE CONCEPT OF DIALOGIC FORM

Sonata Theory and Dialogic Form

James Hepokoski

The analytical procedure that we call Sonata Theory rethinks several postulates of traditional music analysis.[1] While it adopts the precision-language of current music theory, its reprocessing of core analytical issues is also informed by broader work in literary criticism and philosophy: genre theory, phenomenological and reader-response theory, hermeneutics, and others. The result blends close analytical description with the larger perspectives of continental criticism. While I cannot lay out the system or even a sufficient number of its essential concepts in any brief essay, I can at least illustrate a few of its central modes of thinking.

The most basic question at stake when we deal with our own concretizations of musical structure or when we seek to build systems of formal classification is: what is 'form' itself? What might we mean, on a small scale, when we say that a certain phrase of music *is* a period or a sentence or (in William E. Caplin's terms) *is* a hybrid between the two? On a larger scale, what do we mean when we say that a work is *in* a certain form (like sonata form, rondo form, and so on)? How one constructs an answer to such issues determines how one approaches formally any piece of music. It is at this fundamental level that Sonata Theory proposes a new orientation.

In what follows I single out two of its basic principles. First, I note that perceptions of form are as much a collaborative enterprise of the listener or analyst as they are of the composer. And second, I suggest that grasping the full range of an implicit musical form is most essentially a task of reconstructing a processual dialogue between any individual work (or section thereof) and the charged network of generic norms, guidelines, possibilities, expectations, and limits provided by the implied genre at hand. This is 'dialogic form:' form in dialogue with historically conditioned compositional options. From today's standpoint these are earlier periods' now-eclipsed horizons of expectations that we are obliged to recover through sensitive and patient reconstruction. Dialogic form stands in sharp distinction to two other, more traditional categories of formal description. One of these (to use Mark Evan Bonds's terminology) is 'conformational form:' form understood as conforming to a model. (That is emphatically not the approach of Sonata Theory, which, with its interest in formal deformations, does not insist on any necessity to 'conform.') The other is 'generative form:' the conviction that form is generated primarily from the developing motivic processes or contrapuntal work inlaid uniquely into the piece.[2] Of the two categories, generative form has been far more in the ascendancy in the past half-century, but even while aspects of its method are appealing and relevant, that category, too, especially when embraced as an analytical dogma to the exclusion of other factors, differs from the way that we construe form.[3]

The Sonata-Theory method proposes that the form of any individual composition is neither wholly contained nor self-defined by the acoustic happenings within that piece alone. Even while agreeing that our historically informed recognition of varied recurrences of culturally sanctioned, flexible patterns within single musical works is crucially important as a first step in analysis (one should not mistake a straightforward minuet-and-trio for a theme-and-variations, a development for a recapitulation, a sentence for a period), this concept insists that our understanding of form must not be limited to that. Form is not exclusively a property of the individual piece, an attribute to be uncovered once and for all by the analyst as a substantive thing, nor it is only an abstract shape or *ad hoc* design to be charted or culled from the work's audible surface—a mere set of descriptive data (however accurate), a linear massing of statistics, a graph. Instead, the deeper sense of form with which we are concerned here is something to be produced—an engaged act of understanding—through a dialogue with an intricate and subtle network of piece-appropriate norms and guidelines (rules of the game) both for constructing compositions (the concern of the composer) and then for grasping how the composer was likely to have wished us to construe what he or she accomplished in the individual piece under consideration. Listeners also create dialogic form in their own nonclosed dialogues with individual works.

This reorientation alters both the kinds of questions that we ask of music and the way that we talk about formal matters. Its newer aspects can be placed into a higher relief by examining extreme cases. While dialogic form applies to all musical format systems (it can inform our encounters with all of the standardized forms), for the present I shall exemplify the idea primarily with sonata-form construction. What follows considers the structures of three overtures, each of which falls short of realizing some of the most critical features of traditional definitions of sonata form. The first is Beethoven's *Egmont* Overture. The second and third, more extravagant, are Mozart's Overture to *Idomeneo* and Beethoven's Overture to *Die Ruinen von Athen*. Relevant to the whole question at hand is our awareness that while overtures in this period were normatively—almost invariably—construed in dialogue with what we now call sonata form (I shall return to this point below), their often-explicitly dramatic or quasi-representational motivations sometimes led to strikingly free, even extravagant, treatments of individual aspects of the sonata-form layout-options.

I have discussed the ramifications of the *Egmont* problem in a separate study,[4] but in brief this overture's sonata-space displays an orthodox exposition but a recapitulation that brings back and sustains the secondary theme not in the tonic but in the 'wrong key' (see Figure 2.1). The exposition's two tonal planes are the expected F minor and A-flat major (i and III), but the recapitulation's two keys are not F minor and F major but rather F minor and D-flat major (i and VI). The tonal correction back to F major occurs only in the utopian, post-sonata-space laid out in the *Siegessymphonie* coda. *Egmont*'s nonresolving recapitulation violates a cardinal element of what are usually regarded as traditional academic conceptions of sonata form, violates the 'sonata principle' itself—a supposedly sonata-defining principle that centers around the recapitulatory return in the tonic of the originally nontonic secondary theme.[5] Moreover, to the extent that we think that sonata form is most adequately defined tonally, rather than rhetorically or thematically, the problem becomes even more pressing.

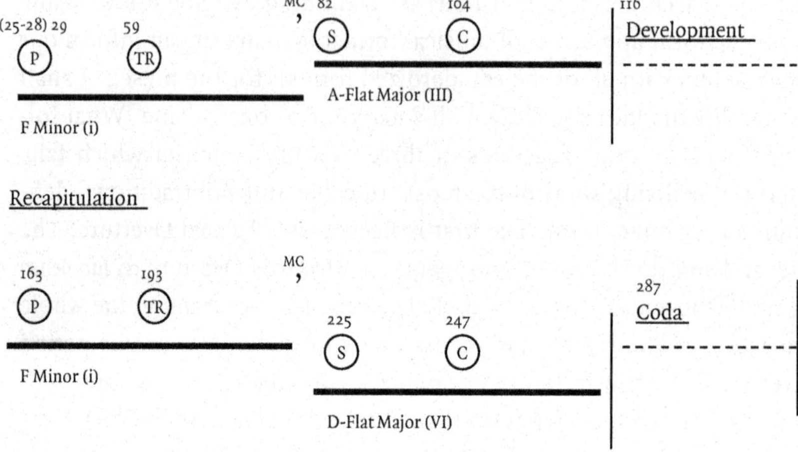

Figure 2.1 Ludwig van Beethoven, Overture to *Egmont*, Op. 84

Does this mean that *Egmont*, lacking this strongly normative tonal resolution within sonata-space,[6] is not a sonata—that Beethoven, in 1808-1809, structured the overture into a unique or completely nongeneric form? Of course not. But what is the analytical interaction that we are expected to have with such a non-normative tonal structure? It is obvious that Beethoven, probably for plot and programmatic reasons that I have laid out elsewhere, invited his listeners to deploy normative sonata-form expectations (like tonal resolution) so that they might perceive a sonic succession that he had here purposefully fashioned to go wrong. In other words, while *Egmont* is not an illustrative sonata according to most of our now-standardized textbook descriptions—indeed, even as it contravenes tonal-definitional sonata principles—we are expected to use our knowledge of sonata-form norms to grasp the aberrations that Beethoven presents to us on its acoustic surface. *Egmont* is set into a dialogue with sonata-form norms even though it does not realize all of them in standard ways. One of our tasks as listeners is to determine where and to what degree the gaps lie between what normally happens in sonata forms and what actually happens here—and then to reflect on the implications of the entire structure placed before us.

Coming to this understanding depends on the listener's negotiation between previously internalized normative expectations and a deformational acoustic surface that features passages willfully transgressive of those norms. The form ultimately perceived—dialogic form—is the product of that negotiation, set into motion by the listener or analyst. The question is not: "Is *Egmont* in sonata form?"—or "Is the *Egmont* Overture a sonata?". Those are the wrong questions, and posed so bluntly they can elicit only wrong or clumsy responses. The more rewarding, dialogical question is: "Are we invited to use our knowledge of the broad range of sonata-form norms and guidelines to interpret what does happen in *Egmont*?". The answer, obviously, is "yes." But to answer "yes" is to imply a different conception of what form is—a different conception (form as interactive dialogue) with significant implications for all analytical work in this area.

Let's pursue the same line of reasoning with a more extreme formal deformation, one from almost three decades earlier—Mozart's D-major overture to *Idomeneo* from 1781 (see Figure 2.2). Here we encounter a largely normative exposition, beginning in D major and leading to a multi-sectional secondary-theme space in the expected dominant, A minor (mm. 45–46), then A major (m. 64). This secondary-theme space is articulated as a 'trimodular block,' a strategy built around double medial caesuras: hence the designations TM^1, TM^2, and TM^3 in the figure.[7] The exposition is followed by a brief, essentially retransitional developmental space (mm. 82–92). But in the expected recapitulation Mozart provides us with only the primary theme and the beginning of the transition in D major, whereupon the recapitulation proper is completely abandoned—no symmetrical secondary-theme-space (or TM^1, TM^2, and TM^3)—and Mozart brings the overture to an end with a brief but thorough recomposition concluding on an expectant V of G minor, the overture's tonic D having now been reprocessed into an active dominant that anticipates the anchoring key of the opening operatic number, Ilia's aria *Padre, germani, addio!*[8]

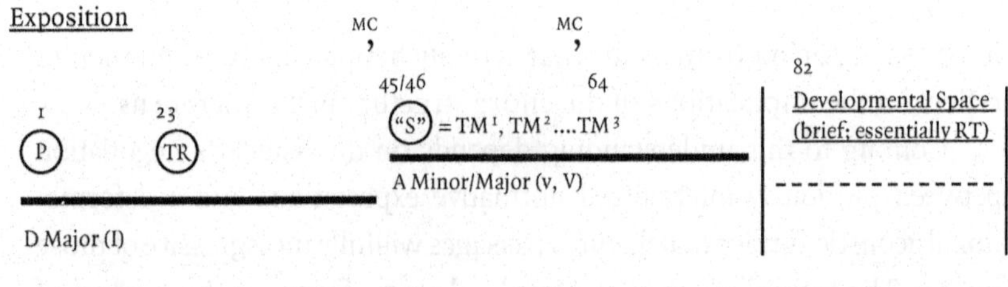

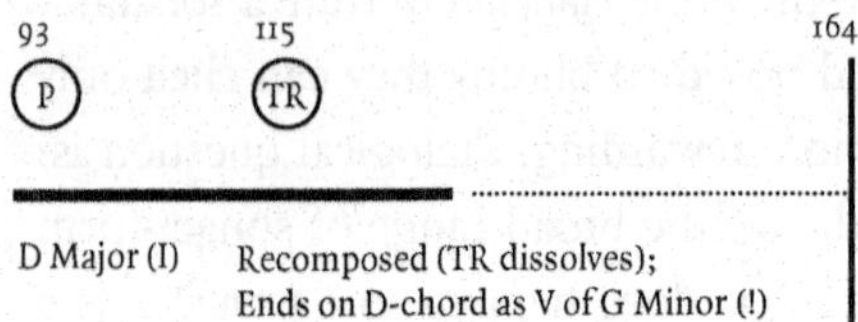

Figure 2.2 Wolfgang Amadeus Mozart, Overture to *Idomeneo*, K. 366

Here we are faced with a 'truncated recapitulation' (producing what amounts to a sonata abandoned three-quarters of the way through, an incomplete sonata or 'sonata fragment')—a truncated recapitulation lacking its definitional second half, that very portion that, through tonal resolution, is supposed to define what we imagine a sonata form to be.[9] While the acoustic surface of the piece does not articulate a complete sonata form, it is clear that we are to grasp the drastic, even violent dialogue that it is having with normative sonata expectations. Again, merely to ask the reductive question, is the *Idomeneo* Overture *in* sonata form, is to miss the point. The actual form, the 'dialogic form,' is concretized—negotiated—by the listener in that gap between what one literally hears and what one understands to be the normative range of options and choices available within the genre of sonata form in its historicized, 1781, Austro-Germanic version, particularly as personally customized by Mozart.

That Mozart, for whatever reason, has given us an only partial, aborted sonata is very much to the essence of whatever that overture might be about, what it might seek to suggest, dramatize, or represent with regard to the (neo)classical, postwar drama that immediately follows. Is it to be construed, as we might conjecture, as a metaphorical image of the repetitive besieging and eventual destruction of the proud walls of Troy? Or might the truncated structure be construed as a musical analogue to the catastrophic storm and shipwreck that had just brought the young Trojan princess Ilia to the island of Crete? Or might it be perhaps grasped as both—a sonic pointing toward the whole catalogue of classical wreckage and collapse that, as a foundational backdrop assumed to be understood by the audience, precedes the opening of the curtain onto Ilia's anxiety and mourning in Act 1, Scene 1? Conceptually matched with a grand and tragic antique-classicism, such peril-filled and destructive images might also be reinforced by such details as the ominous minor-mode mixture that menacingly infiltrates the primary-thematic zone shortly after the work's majestic opening bars, along with the unexpected shift to the suddenly negative A minor—not A major—for the TM[1] onset of secondary-theme space at m. 45, following a 'blocked medial caesura' at m. 41.[10] However we choose to work our way through such considerations, the larger point is that a musical structure of this kind is not a blind or neutralized abstraction, an inert pattern, but is inextricably linked through the process of compositional decision—and especially within overtures—with implications of metaphorical content. Awareness of dialogic structure and the enticing option of formal deformation inevitably leads one into more trenchant matters of hermeneutic interpretation.

With the structure of the *Idomeneo* Overture in mind we now turn to a more challenging but not unrelated work, one with which we shall have to spend more time. In Beethoven's G-major Overture to *Die Ruinen von Athen* from 1811 the deformational notches are ratcheted further away from the typical behavior of any normative sonata. As a result the problem of architectonic implication is more strained: does the multiplicity of unusual features now cross the line at which any sonata-based (dialogic) reading seems inappropriate? I think that it does not, but to demonstrate why requires some close, nuanced reasoning. Without a firm grasp of structural-backdrop or dialogic-form essentials—such as generic precedents and the accepted range of architectural options within overtures—and without a clear view of the process of the overture as a whole it is easy to misread the formal connotations of what the composer gives us here.

We might start by provisionally inquiring into the viability of an interpretation that seeks to construe the unusual work along sonata-form lines—the lines that we would normally anticipate in initially confronting any Beethoven overture. After all, once past its bipartite G-minor/G-major introduction, its large-shape format (see Figure 2.3) resembles that of the sonata-torso of the *Idomeneo* Overture: exposition, development, and truncated recapitulation, this last lacking any return of the secondary and closing zones. Or have we already misconstrued this? An examination of the sonata-form problematics at hand serves as a perfect illustration of the modes of analytical questioning undertaken within dialogic form.

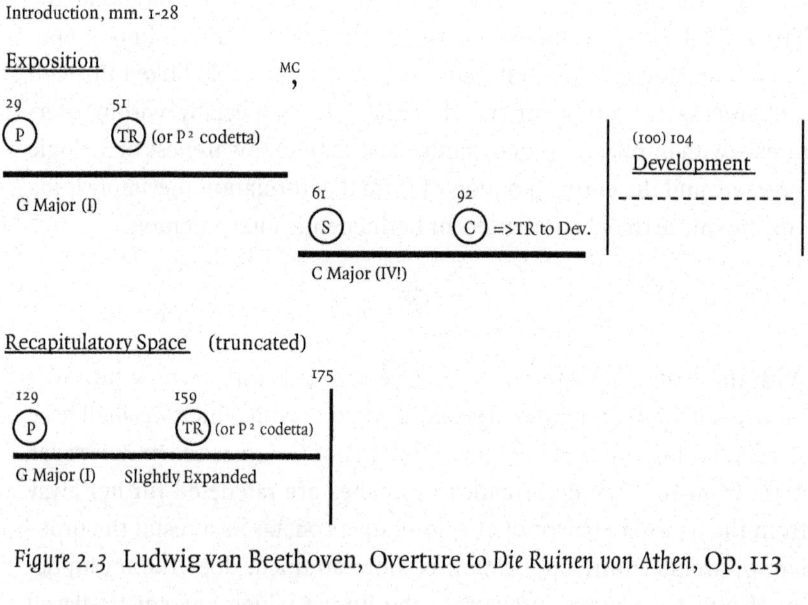

Introduction, mm. 1-28

Exposition

MC

29 P

51 TR (or P² codetta)

G Major (I)

61 S

92 C =>TR to Dev.

C Major (IV!)

(100) 104 Development

Recapitulatory Space (truncated)

129 P

159 TR (or P² codetta)

175

G Major (I) Slightly Expanded

Figure 2.3 Ludwig van Beethoven, Overture to *Die Ruinen von Athen*, Op. 113

Assessing the persuasiveness of drawing out any sonata-form dialogue in this overture is deeply complicated by three factors, all of which precede the development section. First, Beethoven juxtaposed what (in a sonata-oriented reading) we would surely regard as the tonic-key P-block (mm. 29–60) with the non-tonic S-block (mm. 61–92) in an unmediated way. That is, he suppressed traditional transition behavior and medial-caesura preparation and execution—unmistakable features in the overtures to *Idomeneo* and *Egmont*—in favor of a direct juxtaposition of the tonic-key, codetta-like second part of the primary theme (P^2, mm. 51–60) with a completely new theme (m. 61). Retrospectively, it is possible to construe this tonic P^2 as doing double-duty as TR leading to a tonic-key caesura-gap (m. 60; I:PAC MC, a fourth-level default—and thus a very rare selection—within standard MC options),[11] but this kind of direct block-juxtaposition is unusual in Beethoven, and its oddity should not be minimized.

Second, more troublesome, Beethoven chose to sound both the subsequent new theme (our potential S-theme, m. 61) and the closing idea (our potential C, m. 92) not in the usual dominant but rather in the ultra-unorthodox subdominant, C major (IV of the tonic G). This emphatic move to the flat-side—and in this case, a sudden swerve into IV—is traditionally understood as unacceptably out-of-place within sonata expositions, which by definition and tradition are expected to do the opposite, moving instead more tensely sharpward (although of course we may also find a handful of later, Schubertian experiments along these lines).[12] Moreover, this sole candidate for secondary-theme status compounds the tonal strangeness by consistently tilting toward its *own* subdominant—toward the F chord, IV of the already-subdominant C. The exposition as a whole—still under the provisional hypothesis that it is in dialogue with expositional norms—ends unequivocally in IV, C major. Tonally, everything seems inverted, upside-down—flatward motions displacing normatively *de rigueur* sharpward ones.[13]

Third, the subdominant-grounded S-idea (mm. 61–92) is deployed in an unusually closed, rounded-binary format, aa'ba''–ba'' in the manner of a self-contained lyric episode (though without notational repeat-signs) instead of the more commonly loosely constructed or multimodular S typical of the period.[14] The arrestingly counter-normative aspects of this sealed-off lyric design raise significant problems for any frictionlessly claimed secondary-theme understanding of this passage, especially when the appeal is made to sonata-form norms before 1820. (Weber's Overture to *Preciosa* of 1821 provides a briefer, complementary example, albeit from a decade later.) Additionally, while this roundedness and closure might not itself be the decisive factor with regard to formal-role assessment, we should note that its sense of near-utter separateness is also underpinned notationally with an emphatic double-bar at m. 61 and an explicit change of key-signature, signs that more normally flag the onsets of episodes, not secondary themes. In other words, mm. 61–92 display neither the formal nor the notational signs of a standard secondary theme of the time. For the analyst of form, these are problematic issues, ones not easily navigated through.

In short, by the time that we reach the C-major cadence in m. 92 our initial sonata-form expectations—grounded in Mozart's and Beethoven's virtually invariable overture-practice—have been starkly challenged (indeed, placed into confusion, perhaps doubt) by a number of pronounced musical features that proceed counter to that format. Up to that point we have had no fewer than four separate, quasi-encased, thematically contrasting sections, some of which have programmatic connotations. The first is the initial *Andante con moto* in G minor, mm. 1–19, itself subdivided into a murky, diminished-seventh-laden double-gesture, followed by a melodic citation (a 'prolepsis,' mm. 11–19) of a variant of what will be the incidental music's No. 2 to follow, a duet—in this politicized drama—for a 'Greek man and woman,' *Ohne Verschulden Knechtschaft dulden*, an image of contemporary Greece groaning in bondage under the Turks. The second, led by a solo oboe, is a brief, G-major *Marcia moderato* foretaste, mm. 20–28, of the march and chorus of No. 6, *Schmückt die Altäre*, whose later text suggests the hopeful preparations of the altars (decking them, spreading incense, picking roses, awaiting the arrivals) for a day and time of deliverance. The third, with its suddenly quickened, new-launch onset into the G-major *Allegro, ma non troppo*, mm. 29–60—not a quotation from the subsequent incidental music—is what we have been suggesting might serve the role of a P^1–P^2 complex occupying the first part of a sonata exposition.[15] And the fourth—likewise an idea confined to the overture alone—is the C-major subsequent, rounded-binary theme in the subdominant, mm. 61–92, set off by a double bar and a change of key signature.

By m. 92—if not already by m. 61 and its unexpected plunge into the subdominant and a new theme—we might suspect that sonata norms are not the ones operative in this overture, that we ought not to be measuring dialogically what we hear against the more standard procedures of the sonata tradition. Given Beethoven's overture-predilections in the past—not to mention the larger tradition within which he was working—this possibility can strike us as a puzzle, perhaps even a shock. As we assess this situation, the only reasonable conceptual-generic alternative within Beethoven's cultural circle in 1811 would be that of the potpourri (or medley) overture, a loosely chained succession (not sonata-oriented) of quasi-closed melodic previews of the incidental music to come, with perhaps one or more melodies unique to the overture.[16] While by no means frequently encountered in continental overtures of the pre-1811 period—they became more common only in later years—they certainly did exist, most notably, it seems, within some French operas, such as that found in the programmatic hunt-depiction in Méhul's overture to *Le Jeune Henri* (1797), well-known at the time, or the same composer's patently sectionalized overture to *Joseph* (1807).[17] The format, in any event, was known to the period as a looser, more casual structural option for some kinds of (perhaps lighter? or non-Austro-Germanic?) overtures.

At least by m. 92 this option squares with the musical facts on the ground so far, and it might help to ease our concerns both about the fourth melodic event's occupation of the subdominant, C major (mm. 61–92), and about its closed-episodic shape, double-bar separation, and new key signature. On the other hand, the potpourri-overture format is one that does not appear elsewhere in Beethoven—or in Mozart, Haydn, Cherubini, or Weber, for that matter (though one might point to the programmatic, sectionally concatenated structure of the 'exceptional' *Wellingtons Sieg* from 1813—only two years later and another occasional piece—as a rough analogue).[18] Had Beethoven decided to enter into a dialogue with that format uniquely for this overture, that would have been a startlingly counter-normative choice. And that choice would have to be confronted in any analytical encounter with this music. Merely to suggest *en passant* the piece's potpourri nature and to let it go at that—as if the problem were so readily solved—would be to evade the central expressive question that the overture poses. Beethoven's conscious adoption of a (for him) unique, non-normative overture-format would demand from us a hermeneutic or interpretive explanation, presumably one relevant to the drama that the overture sought to introduce, unless we are prepared to suggest, as we should not be, that the overture's structure and content were, for whatever reason, randomly or casually assembled. Neither the nature of the commissioned occasion nor aspects of compositional haste or disregard can be adduced here. The incidental music for *Die Ruinen von Athen* was composed in 1811, along with the *König Stephan* incidental music, for the official opening in early 1812 of the German-language Royal Theater in Pest. Beethoven crafted its sibling piece, the overture to *König Stephan*, in an unambiguous sonata form. Why not, then, in *Die Ruinen von Athen*?

Whatever we might make of the potpourri option, its viability recedes markedly with what follows after m. 100. An impetuous tonal lurch into m. 99 provides a strongly articulated half-cadence caesura on V of A minor (ii of G; vi of C), and mm. 100–04 feature a flute-led, sunshiny entry-link in A major (with change of key signature) to the filling of a brief developmental space in mm. 104–24. In other words, more characteristically generic signs of sonata-ness now take over. While the developmental space is anything but extended—indeed, it is so short and unelaborated as almost to merit consideration as an expanded retransition—its rudimentary (half-hearted?) developmental signs are nonetheless evident. It is half-rotational (P-based, as is the norm for onsets of developments),[19] leading the initial P-head-motive by elementary descending fifths toward the eventual G-tonic-recovery in locally broad, Beethovenian strides: A major (m. 104), A minor (m. 108, 'lights out'), and V^7 (m. 112, a dominant-lock pulsating also with a $^6_4$ upper neighbor), which last chord-lock pushes with a mighty *fortissimo* thrust (mm. 120–24) toward a fermata-sustained, expectant V^7 in m. 124.

What we had once considered (by m. 92) might have been a potpourri-succession of episodic tunes, then, has now sported a typical 'developmental space,' and after four bars of caesura-fill (mm. 125–28) what follows is obviously a full, methodical 'recapitulation' in the tonic of the first *allegro, ma non troppo* theme (carried at complete length, albeit with minor alterations)—our P^1+P^2 complex—which, once sounded and only very slightly extended, brings the overture to a close. In sum, the presence of a developmental space and truncated recapitulation (as well as the slow or separate introduction followed by the *Allegro ma non troppo*) ought to swing our thoughts round again to that of a sonata deformation—and we might again consider at this point both the *Idomeneo* precedent and yet also the stark, counter-generic differences with which this Beethoven overture presents us.

While the developmental space and truncated recapitulation suggest that the sonata category of norms is to be considered the more fundamental, we might be advised to formulate an adequately nuanced description of this unusual structure—to *explicate the ambiguity*, as opposed to rigidly declaring on behalf of any single form. In *Die Ruinen von Athen* Beethoven's *primary* dialogue, as we learn by the end of the piece (once having experienced the telltale development and recapitulation of P^1+P^2, surely the most crucial features guiding our final sense of this anomalous structure as a whole), is with sonata norms. More specifically, he is engaged in a dialogue with the truncated-recapitulation variant of it. We enter the overture with sonata-form expectations (on the basis of our historical experience, at least initially confirmed with the separate introduction leading to an *allegro, ma non troppo* launch), and those expectations are reinforced, however deformationally, by the end. Along the way, though—and especially in the problematic mm. 61–92 domains (those containing the subdominant, rounded-binary melody)—we may be invited to consider that Beethoven might instead have been basing his overture on a different generic practice, that of the potpourri or melodic-succession overture—a more casual strategy normally alien to his overtures and hence puzzling here. By the end of the piece, however, it seems most reasonable—and flexible—to conclude that the early and transient potpourri effect, if intended as such, represented only a potential *secondary* generic dialogue, a substantial flicker of generic doubt, encountered along the way. In sum, the reading proposed here is that Beethoven invites us in the latter portions of the first half of the piece to consider whether he might be engaging in that *secondary* dialogue with the looser, less rigorous potpourri format only to correct such impressions midstream (or to regard them as only secondary) by nuancing the overture into a more generically elevated, if still deformationally incomplete sonata-format.

So eccentric is the structure of *Die Ruinen von Athen*—which has been a frequently marginalized or dismissed work in Beethoven studies—that it is difficult to find any significant pronouncement upon it within the analytical literature. With its local potpourri effects, with its emphatic tonic-closure of P^1 and P^2 (lacking normative signs of a transitional move toward S), with its wrong-key, rounded-binary 'episodic' secondary theme (is it a secondary theme at all?), and with its truncated recapitulation, how can we identify this as any kind of sonata form, whose norms it contravenes right and left? But again, from our perspective, this is the wrong question. The question instead is, at the end of the day are we *primarily* to interpret whatever odd happenings that we find in *Die Ruinen von Athen* according to the lights provided by our own reconstruction today of the interpretive guidelines of normative sonata form—thus registering the overture's transgressions as real transgressions or deformations of generic norms? My preferred answer is "yes:" from the dialogical perspective, at least, *Die Ruinen von Athen* can be heard as an extreme sonata deformation, albeit one also sporting the apparent potpourri nuances acknowledged above.

Such an interpretative reading—by no means a declaration of a finally uncovered 'fact'—is rooted in our foreknowledge of established genres as enablers of discourse. As mentioned above, dramatic and operatic overtures of this period, including overtures written as incidental music to plays or ballets—and certainly Beethoven's—were almost invariably written in dialogue with sonata-form norms. To write a serious *allegro*-tempo overture was to place oneself in dialogue with sonata-form procedures as the overwhelming formal expectation. (The later *Die Weihe des Hauses* from 1822 would be a rare exception—a composition, we might recall, that was a replacement for the *Die Ruinen von Athen* Overture in the context of a somewhat modified revival of much of the original incidental music.)[20] To the sonata-form-based overture there was only one structural alternative in 1811: what we now call the potpourri overture. Other large-scale formats that might cast themselves up as abstract possibilities—rondos, for instance, or ABA' formats—were not structures that were deployed within fast-tempo overtures. Put another way, *they were not generically available for use within such overtures*. No knowledgeable listener would (or should) 'go into' any *allegro*-tempo overture of the period with the possibility, for example, of a rondo-format in mind. Realizing the sheer nonavailability of that format in this situation provides part of the indispensable backdrop for any dialogic reading of the structure of *Die Ruinen von Athen*. Genre-expectations are an essential feature of the dialogic conception of form. One should never read (or chart) an acoustic-surface pattern or portion thereof in the abstract, without regard to these historical expectations and availabilities. This is one feature that sets dialogic form apart from its alternatives. Or, conversely, if a composer, in 1811, did decide to make the extraordinary decision to override all generic expectations by producing, say, a rondo, completely outside the normative realm of structural options for an overture—which is certainly not the case here—one might expect that that structure and thematic types would at least have to be as clear and unmistakable as possible, precisely in order to perceive clearly that unusual choice. But *Die Ruinen von Athen*, as a whole, articulates no unambiguous rondo-shape, particularly in light of its developmental space and truncated recapitulation. Consequently, what might be our temptation to read the strong local resemblance of the subdominant-key, rounded-binary mm. 61–92 to a typical, off-tonic rondo-episode is misguided, even if, as a purely local effect, and in the abstract, our present-day thoughts might turn initially—though only momentarily—in that direction.[21] (I shall return below to the equally problematic ABA' consideration.)

Once we interpret the structure, dialogically, as primarily a sonata deformation (with secondary complications), the question then becomes: why did Beethoven write it as such? The challenge is thrown down to his listeners—to *us*—as those concretizers of dialogic structure and its potential for hermeneutic implication.

We might start with an awareness of Kotzebue's original plot for the one-act stage-play, *Die Ruinen von Athen*, along with a knowledge of the eight numbers of incidental music that follow. These concern Greece's then-current bondage under Turkish rule (presented as the despoiling of an originary and exemplary antique culture) and the resultant recovery of this classical past through the triumphant transferal of the spirit of antique glory to the German-speaking urban centers of the Habsburg *imperium*—or, in the Hungarian context of this play, specifically to Pest. With this in mind we might be tempted to suggest that the tonal inversion of the exposition (tonality as if viewed through a reversing mirror, with normatively sharpward motion inversionally reflected flatward) might have something to do with the ground-concept of reflecting backward into a remote and distant (or even pastoral?) Hellenic antiquity (only dimly perceptible from the dawning nineteenth-century present, and in the midst of a growing German-language interest in Hellenism).[22] Similarly, the truncated recapitulation might reasonably be associated with the classical image of 'fragments' or 'ruins'—once-whole things, *Die Ruinen von Athen*, with an arm or a leg or a crucial arch or support-pedestal once there but now lost forever. Or, under slightly different lights, the pointedly 'nonintegrated' nature (or potpourri aspect) of the first four themes might be taken to suggest near-inert raw materials—musically modular things, as it were—the beginning steps of whose integration and interaction are taken only with the not-fully-realized sonata process that only weakly begins to shape the scattered and disparate, noninteractive parts into the Austrian-Empire whole represented not only by the sonata process but also by the context of the ceremonial occasion of the celebration in Pest. In other words, the structure and literal performance of the piece itself enact the process of assimilating 'fragments' and 'ruins' into a workable, quasi-integrated whole through the execution of the musical event—this overture—which is taking place as a celebratory event, in real time, in German-language (Austrian-Empire) Pest.

As it happens, the structural deformation that we find in both *Idomeneo* and *Die Ruinen von Athen* (no recapitulatory appearance of the secondary theme; a recapitulation aborted at the primary-theme or transition-point), both images of antique-classical wreckage—perhaps not coincidentally—is not unique to those two compositions. It is rare, though, to find a truncated recapitulation in *allegro*-tempo compositions. On the other hand, we do encounter it more frequently in slow movements, where (as some have noted) it might suggest something of a hybrid between a sonata form and a ternary, ABA' form, especially when, as is most common, a developmental space is lacking.[23] Such truncated-recapitulation slow movements can be found for instance in two of Haydn's quartets from Op. 33 (Nos. 5 and 6), in his Piano Trio in E-flat (Hob. XV:30), in Mozart's Quartet in D (K. 575) and his Piano Concerto in A (K. 488), and in Beethoven's Piano Concerto No. 1 in C (Op. 15), and his Septet in E-flat (Op. 20).[24] In other words, what is especially remarkable about *Idomeneo* and *Die Ruinen von Athen* is that the torso-structure is encountered, non-normatively, within full-scale *allegro*-tempo works, where amplitude of form and intent, including developmental activity, is much more normally the formal imperative.[25]

Realizing that the sonata deformations that we find in *Idomeneo* and *Die Ruinen von Athen* participate in a broader network of truncated-recapitulation works suggests still another feature of Sonata Theory analysis. That is, works of music do not exist as isolated monads generating their formal meanings exclusively from within. On the contrary, every work throws out multiple threads of intertextual connection to other, similar pieces, works socially remembered, possible classic models, in-play influential procedures, and so on. Every work—a sonata, a symphony, an individual movement, and an individual passage—is but a single node within a reticulate, multidimensional network—socially accumulative—of other works within and outside of its genre. The single work incites inquiries not merely into its own idiosyncratic meaning—what I refer to as an individualized meaning or 'immanent meaning' particular only to the piece itself—but also into what I call its 'relational meaning,' that is, the social meaning resulting from its situated position in a complex network of comparable and not comparable pieces within the field of cultural production available to the composer at the time of composition. In other words, one aspect of the meaning of the overture to *Die Ruinen von Athen* resides in how Beethoven situated that musical product—or how we now situate it—within a real *Sitz im Leben* (or life-situation) in which cultural status, art-claim expertise, and social prestige are at stake. Relational meaning is concerned with investigating how such a piece seeks to occupy a socially charged position in relation to other works within the larger field of cultural production. Such considerations broaden the notion of what form and content (or varying types of socially construed meaning) might be.

My illustration of the idea has been through examples of distortions of standard forms, ones so notable that they may at first seem to contravene the most basic requirements of the culturally received form: *Egmont*, *Idomeneo*, *Die Ruinen von Athen*. But this is not to imply that only deformational or anamorphic forms are dialogic. On the contrary (to remain within the realm of sonata form), even the most standard of sonatas—the first movement, say, of Mozart's *Eine kleine Nachtmusik*—exemplifies dialogic form insofar as its moment-to-moment particulars are equally engaged in a dialogue with the hierarchical array of generic options that we now call sonata form. It is only that its architectonic choices are more normative. But we as listeners are nonetheless invited to reconstruct its generic dialogue in our own minds. Any individually texturized and shaped acoustic surface, normative or not, provides us with a succession of compositional choices that ask to be viewed through the lens of whatever network of formal norms we knowledgeably decide to be appropriate to the task. If we do not use the proper generic interpretive lens for the piece in question (that is, if we misjudge the pre-existing formal network with which the piece is in dialogue), then the piece will be puzzling, perhaps making no sense whatever.

As a *reductio ad absurdum*—and to state the obvious: Were we, for whatever reason, perversely to take up the wrong interpretive lens—say, that of 'theme and variations' or fugue—little that we find in the opening movement of *Eine kleine Nachtmusik* would make the slightest sense. It is only our knowledge of sonata practice that permits us to provide the coherence and familiar continuity that we seek within this piece. This may be obvious enough in Mozart, but it commonly happens in later music, where the fundamental generic-norm backdrop can be, often mistakenly, a matter of dispute—in analyzing, say, some finales of Brahms, some first movements of Mahler, or some tone poems of Strauss, cases where the degree of deviation from socially entrenched norms is precisely the point—that selecting the wrong analytical lens has led more than one analyst into a deeply mistaken discussion. In confronting such later, complex music, one's sense of implied formal norms and generic dialogues needs to be informed by a strong historical knowledge of what the likely options at that point in time actually were, along with what types of continuity with earlier norms one might or might not expect to encounter.

By way of conclusion, I might note only that the concept of dialogic form is by no means limited to sonatas, though that has been the format that I have chosen to discuss here, and that is the format with which the *Elements of Sonata Theory* was most concerned. Prior to my own sonata work I had worked out the basics of the dialogic concept within Italian opera, that is, within the *ottocento* aria-, duet-, and ensemble-practice of Bellini,

Donizetti, Verdi, and others. What I came to realize was that the same concept is applicable and immediately liberating in our discussions of all musical forms at all moments of history—the many dialogical variants of da capo aria, fugue, rondo, chorale-prelude, popular music formats, blues formats, sentence and period formats, and so on.

But all of this is to suggest larger issues of conception and classification. For the present I conclude only by noting that while the concept of dialogic form is disarmingly easy to grasp as a grounding procedure of analysis, what it leads to, once absorbed, is nothing less than a reorientation in how we approach the understanding of all of our standard forms—a reorientation that is more flexible, more intuitive, and more responsive to the way that such forms operate in concrete, socially interactive practice.

Comments on James Hepokoski's Essay "Sonata Theory and Dialogic Form"

William E. Caplin

In his essay, James Hepokoski makes a persuasive case that his preferred analytical methodology—'dialogic form'—offers significant advantages over earlier procedures, such as the 'conformational' and 'generative' approaches identified by Mark Evan Bonds [>72].[1] As Hepokoski clearly shows, a dialogic approach powerfully engages an articulated theoretical background with a flexible analytical application in ways that highlight the formal individuality of a musical work. And his moving beyond purely formal explanations into the realm of hermeneutic analysis enriches his methodology all the more.

Indeed, I am sympathetic to Hepokoski's dialogic approach and believe that my own analyses largely follow the spirit of that enterprise. Seeing as my theory of formal functions is based on a wide-spread empirical study of a restricted musical repertory, focused around the works of three composers within a limited geographical and temporal context (Vienna, roughly 1770–1810), the formal categories that I identify effectively embody the "norms, guidelines, possibilities, expectations, and limits" of a clearly defined historical background [>71].[2] Any analytical application of my theory will by necessity carry with it the caveat 'in relation to classical practice' and thus bring forth elements of the dialogical processes advocated by Hepokoski. (That I rarely extend my concerns to hermeneutic considerations is due to my own scholarly inclinations rather than to any methodological qualms, though, as I suggest toward the end of these comments, a hermeneutic interpretation is only as solid as the formal analyses upon which it is based.)

A central issue for any dialogic analysis is the choice of categories against which to assess the formal manifestation of a particular work (usually, just a single movement). As I argued in my opening essay, I find it advantageous to focus on categories of formal function rather than formal type, and I see such advantages playing out in the three overtures that Hepokoski analyzes in his essay. For in considering certain phrase-structural situations associated with specific middle-ground formal functions, especially those of 'subordinate theme' and 'development,' I find that his choice of underlying formal type is either problematic or insufficiently exploited. Indeed, I believe it is essential to address levels of phrase functionality, since decisions there directly impinge upon any assessment of large-scale form.[3]

Egmont. Hepokoski's choice of sonata form as the model with which to discover a deformation in this overture strikes me as entirely appropriate. Indeed, it is almost impossible to imagine any other formal type that could have come into consideration. And the deformation of sonata form surely results, in part, from the lack of home-key closure within the recapitulation function itself. Beethoven evidently wanted to forestall a shift to the home-key *major* until the *Siegessymphonie* coda, and so he brought the subordinate theme in the submediant region of the home key; he thus fails to provide any cadential closure for the home key in the confines of the recapitulation proper. As a result, the emphasis on the home-key major of the coda is highly anticipated because of its being withheld in the recapitulation and so enormously satisfying when it finally does appear.[4]

But the matter goes beyond purely tonal considerations. For another deformation of sorts concerns the phrase-structural organization of the subordinate theme itself, both in the exposition and recapitulation. Unusual for a symphonic-style exposition for Beethoven is the relatively 'tight-knit' organization of this theme in relation to the main theme, which itself is quite 'loose,' lacking as it does a proper cadence.[5] Not only is the main theme longer than the subordinate theme (30 measures versus 23), but the latter lacks the typical devices that help provide powerful momentum to the cadential arrival, such as evaded cadences and expanded cadential progressions. Indeed, listeners might wonder whether the norms of tight-knit versus loose organization have been largely upset, so that by the end of the exposition, they will already perceive that something is formally awry, that this is far from an "orthodox" exposition, as Hepokoski contends [>73]. And when the same situation obtains in the recapitulation, listeners may demand all the more for the coda to set things right. And so it does, not only tonally, but also phrase-structurally, by providing the requisite loosening techniques (evaded cadence at m. 301; expanded cadential progressions at mm. 319–23 and 325–29) that were missing from both the exposition and recapitulation, techniques that support the much needed emphasis on the home-key tonic. We see, therefore, that a consideration of the phrase-structural situation, especially in relation to a theory of tight-knit versus loose formal organization, yields an account of sonata deformation that surpasses the manifest tonal irregularities clearly identified by Hepokoski.

Idomeneo. The choice of sonata form as the obvious model against which to uncover the formal irregularities of this overture seems to me, at first glance, problematic. To be sure, a clear exposition is evident; likewise, it is not unreasonable to consider the return of the main theme at m. 93 to signal the start of a recapitulation, though we learn soon enough that this function is not fully realized. Missing entirely, however, is a section that can properly be considered a development. Measures 82–92 have neither the scope, the tonal instabilities, nor the phrase-structural make-up of a genuine development section. Hepokoski correctly identifies a retransitional function associated with these measures, but I would argue that they represent the kind of retransition conventionally associated with the end of an *exposition*, not a development. Thus the formal type that most readily models this overture is 'sonata without development' (Hepokoski and Darcy's sonata Type 1), a form typical of the overture genre.[6]

That being said, there is a way of interpreting this work in terms of sonata form, though differently from that proposed by Hepokoski. We would still hear mm. 82–92 as an expositional retransition, but in this case leading not immediately to the recapitulation, but rather to a written-out repeat of the exposition itself.[7] Striking is the fact that the entire main theme and transition of the exposition are restated exactly (including the identical instrumentation), going even so far as to reach the dominant of the dominant (m. 121), thus proposing again a modulation to the subordinate key. Indeed the music departs from the path of the exposition only at what would have been the beginning of the subordinate theme (m. 127).[8] But rather than repeating the subordinate-theme group, the music leads to an extended passage that features broad model–sequence technique (mm. 137–45; 146–54), exactly what is found in the 'core' of a development.[9] When the music breaks down and finishes off on the dominant of the subdominant, the listener can have the impression that the work has collapsed mid-stream—well within 'developmental space' and much before having even arrived at the recapitulation. Here, then, is a more radical sonata deformation than the truncated recapitulation proposed by Hepokoski. Note that my analyses here depart from those of my colleague largely on the basis of our differing conceptions of development function. Again, an emphasis on formal functionality, particularly at the phrase-structural level, guides my analytical decisions.[10]

Die Ruinen von Athen. Hepokoski marshals a wide range of evidence—theoretical, historical, and hermeneutic—to argue that a sonata-form deformation lies at the heart of this overture. His position, however, remains unconvincing to me. To be sure, two constituent functions of the sonata are recognizable—a main theme and a (highly condensed) development. It is not possible, in my opinion, to find a subordinate theme and, as Hepokoski himself acknowledges, there is no transition. In the absence of these two functions, it is fairly impossible to speak of a sonata exposition (or recapitulation). The unit that Hepokoski identifies as the subordinate theme does not reside in any standard subordinate key,[11] nor is its phrase-structural organization, a clear rounded binary variant (A‖:B–A':‖), at all appropriate for this formal function (as noted by Hepokoski [>84]).

A perfectly acceptable alternative to subordinate theme presents itself, however; namely, that of 'interior theme,' a thematic function associated with the 'large ternary form' and the various 'rondo forms.'[12] Interior themes are normally constructed in relation to the small ternary (rounded binary) theme type, are frequently enough set in the subdominant tonal region (especially in rondos), and are located between two appearances of the main theme (hence their 'interior' quality). The closing cadence of an interior theme typically leads to a retransition: "in the sonata–rondo, this retransition can be highly developmental, even to the extent of resembling a core."[13] Clearly, then, the scheme that emerges following the slow introduction of this overture conforms in its most essential respects to large ternary form, which contains the functions: (1) main theme, (2) interior theme, and (3) return of main theme. That I invoked sonata–rondo form in relation to this particular interior theme (especially its residing in the subdominant and its containing a developmental retransition) does not mean that I find this formal type at the basis of the movement. Rather, this reference exemplifies well a central point that I argued in my opening essay; namely, that an emphasis on formal function rather than formal type allows one to retain a good deal of analytical flexibility while still holding firm to fundamental theoretical principles underlying this style. Thus we can speak of an interior theme without thereby invoking the rondo type as a formal option for the work.[14] To be sure, Hepokoski is correct to assert that neither rondo nor large ternary forms are found in other Beethoven overtures (or even those of his contemporaries). But this should not mean that either formal type is entirely 'unavailable' to the composer (or to the listener). The large ternary form was certainly adopted by him in other instrumental genres and, as corny as it may sound, I am not certain that we should deny the possibility that Beethoven—of all composers—may have exerted a certain 'artistic freedom' in his choice of formal type here. Finally, if the overture is based on the large ternary (and thus can be heard dialogically in reference to that form), then the absence of a genuine recapitulation disallows our speaking of any formal 'truncation.' In that case, a hermeneutic reading founded on such a deformation must be called into doubt. As engaging as Hepokoski's thoughts on the classical image of "'fragments' and 'ruins'" may be [>86], they fail to convince in light of a wholly integrated ternary structure, whose component functions are rendered fully complete.

Hepokoski's dialogic methodology requires him to choose at least one formal type with which the work enters into dialogue. In all three analyses, he has adopted 'sonata form' as the overriding type, though he would be the first to acknowledge that other forms can also come into consideration. Moreover, he would undoubtedly sanction the possibility of employing multiple types to help reveal the individuality of a given work. I, too, endorse the selection of one or more forms against which to assess a work's unique design. My alternative analyses either involve the choice of another form (sonata without development in the case of *Idomeneo*, large ternary for *Die Ruinen von Athen*) or varying ways of employing sonata form (*Egmont*, *Idomeneo*). But even more importantly, our conflicting views are rooted in different conceptions about the formal functions making up the types that are chosen to model the work. In particular, our differing notions of what constitutes the functions of subordinate theme and development account for many of the analytical alternatives discussed in these comments. In the end, fundamental theory—much more than analytical methodology—drives our formal interpretations.

Comments on James Hepokoski's Essay "Sonata Theory and Dialogic Form"

James Webster

James Hepokoski's essay is based on his and Warren Darcy's new and manifestly important treatise *Elements of Sonata Theory*. I shall restrict myself to two brief comments: on his interpretation of the 'sonata principle' (with respect to *Egmont*), and on the concept of 'dialogic form' (with respect to *Die Ruinen von Athen*).

Egmont. The (unfortunately named) 'sonata principle' was introduced by Edward T. Cone in 1968—"important statements made in a key other than the tonic must either be re-stated in the tonic, or brought into a closer relation with the tonic, before the movement ends"—and rapidly became an analytical-critical commonplace, for example in the writings of Charles Rosen and myself.[1] Recently, Hepokoski has subjected it to an elaborate critique (citations in his notes 4 and 5 [>111]), of which many aspects are well-founded, others dubious or overargued. I will focus on Cone's qualification "or brought into a closer relation with the tonic," in the context of *Egmont*. Although Cone gave no examples that are directly pertinent, he clearly had Beethoven's procedure (and other comparable ones) in mind: the second group, originally in A-flat, is recapitulated not in F minor (i–III / i–i) or major (i–III / i–I), but transposed down a fifth, in D-flat (i–III / i–VI). The issue is twofold: (a) To what extent can a transposed but non-tonic recapitulation of significant second-group material count as a resolution within a sonata context? (b) If (as in *Egmont*) the tonic is not restored at all until after the thematic recapitulation, what are the consequences?

(a) Hepokoski's view is that the EEC (I would say 'structural cadence') from the exposition, in order to count as 'essential structural closure' (ESC), must be recapitulated in the tonic. (By extension, this applies to most or all of the significant material from the second group.) However, in the nineteenth century the range of normative recapitulatory key-relationships (like key-relationships generally) was much expanded.[2] The entire second group can be transposed down a fifth (Schubert's String Quintet in C major: I–♭III–V / I–♭VI–I; Brahms's Third Symphony in F Major: I–III–iii / I–VI–vi); or appear in the tonic (often in both modes) when the exposition employed two keys (Schubert's Grand Duo in D major: I–♭VI–V / I–i–I); or be divided between two tonics when the exposition had only one (Brahms's G-Minor Piano Quartet: i–V–v / i–VI–i). If tonic recapitulation were the sole criterion, the (absurd) result would be that in Schubert's String Quintet the middle section of the exposition is not 'really' recapitulated, whereas in the Grand Duo it is! Nor would it help to argue that, since these sections originally stand in neither tonic nor dominant and are therefore tonally 'transitional,' it doesn't matter in what key they are recapitulated; in Schubert and Brahms these sections are constituents of the form, which count as much as the final ones.

The concept "brought into closer relation with the tonic" is not unduly vague or factitious, despite Cone's failure to spell it out. Transposition down a fifth indeed creates a powerful analogy to the V → I relation of the sonata principle, particularly since such a recapitulation usually ends in the tonic, such that the transposed passages become more closely related to that key phenomenologically as well. Another possibility involves a change of mode, as in the second theme of the Grand Duo: C minor is of course a closer relation to C major than A-flat. In the exposition of Brahms's Piano Quartet (above), the second theme appears in the 'paradoxical' dominant major, before the later second group reverts to the diatonic dominant minor; in the recapitulation the diatonic E-flat major is, again, more closely related to the tonic. (From this point of view the occasional transposition a fifth *up*, as in the first movements of Beethoven's quartets Op. 130 and 132 and Schubert's *Unfinished*, might seem more problematic, although in these cases it is ameliorated by the fact that the keys are remote (in Op. 130) or the overall tonic is minor.)

(b) In the great majority of the works under discussion (including all those cited above), the final paragraph or section of the recapitulation, including the ESC (structural cadence), does appear in the tonic. Nevertheless, there are significant works by both Beethoven (*Egmont*; Op. 132) and Brahms (C Minor Piano Quartet; Third Symphony), in which the tonic is not restored until after the thematic recapitulation.

These are admittedly exceptional cases in the context of sonata theory, of any stripe. In Op. 132, in which the entire recapitulation is (again) a fifth *higher* than the exposition (i–VI / v–III), the coda (or coda + second recapitulation, as some have it) restates the main theme, transition theme, and second theme in the tonic—but *not* the closing group. In the Brahms Quartet, the entire second group is recapitulated astonishingly in the dominant major (G major), with a last-minute, catastrophic restoration of C minor in the coda, which (as Tovey pointed out)[3] presumably motivated the otherwise unusual maintenance of the same key in the ensuing *Scherzo*. Especially in light of other extrinsic and intrinsic aspects of both works, hermeneutic interpretation is indeed called for.[4] In Brahms's Third, by contrast, notwithstanding a number of suggestive aspects of the work as a whole, nobody has interpreted its non-tonic recapitulation *as such* in hermeneutic terms, no doubt in part because it closes in the (in this context) 'neutral' key of D minor.[5] Structurally, it was presumably the absence of the dominant as key in the first movement, indeed any structural dominant chord until the coda, that induced Brahms to compensate: C is the tonic of both interior movements, and is unusually prominent, as both note and key, in the finale.

Regarding *Egmont*: of course the tonal disposition of the recapitulation is exceptional, and the delayed return to the tonic is related to the transformative character of the *Siegessymphonie* in F major; and of course all this invites interpretation. In fact, however, the tonic is restored—massively—*before* the change of tempo, at the root-position and *fortissimo* in mm. 275–76, on the way to the structural dominant. Moreover, this passage is a free but unmistakable recomposition of the transition from the end of the *Sostenuto* to the beginning of the *Allegro* (see Figure 2.4): VI–iv–(i)–V, with the dominant prolonged across the tempo-divide (shown in bold-face) and resolving to the tonic only later, *in medias res*. Thus the thematic links between *sostenuto* and *Siegessymphonie* are correlated with harmonic-formal ones.[6]

Sostenuto → *Allegro*	15	19		21	**25**	29
Allegro → *Siegessymphonie*	259	267	275	278/285	**287**	295
	VI	iv	(i)	V ____	____	i or I

Figure 2.4 Ludwig van Beethoven, Overture to *Egmont*, Op. 84: correspondences between *Sostenuto–Allegro* transition and *Allegro–Siegessymphonie* transition

In short, even though (with respect to works in the canon) *Egmont* is (among) the earliest works to have a fully non-resolving recapitulation,[7] I do not believe that this tonal disposition *as such* 'demands' interpretation, any more than in Brahms's Third. Notwithstanding Hepokoski's critique, a recapitulation at the fifth below remains an effective procedure of tonal 'grounding.'

Die Ruinen von Athen. Beethoven's overture is indeed exceptional, both within his 'oeuvre' and in the general turn-of-the-century context. It does not merely 'transgress' sonata(-like) norms while yet perhaps asking to be understood in that generic context, as is the case with *Leonore No.* 2, *Coriolanus*, and (in Hepokoski's view) *Egmont*; rather, it fails, or refuses, to be intelligible in terms of any single formal type. I will comment on the concept 'dialogic form' and on an unacknowledged aesthetic issue.

The issue is not whether 'dialogic form' (and all that it implies) is a viable analytical-critical stance; of course it is. Rather, it is whether the new analytical and hermeneutic (meta-)language and the associated apparatus yield comparably rich analytical benefits.[8] I am not persuaded that this is so. Certainly no concept like 'dialogic form' is required to grasp the formal problematics of Beethoven's overture.[9] Indeed Hepokoski's own analysis, notwithstanding its length and the urgency of his prose, is notably matter-of-fact, although of course he argues that the real work of 'dialogic form' takes place (as it were) on another level, as one assesses a composition in its historical and generic contexts (its "relational meaning" [>87]), and understands its form as fluid and contingent, inflected variously by different listeners and readers. But in this respect as well, I would argue that well-informed historical analyses (if, admittedly, not all analyses in the music-theory world) have always evinced understanding of this kind. Even the role of generic deformation and transgression as an 'invitation' to hermeneutic interpretation, admittedly front-and-center in 'dialogic form,' scarcely requires the latter concept.[10]

The recent (and long overdue) 'turn' in Beethoven studies towards serious consideration of his public music from the first half of the 1810s has by and large focused on issues of history and reception.[11] By contrast, the difficult critical and aesthetic issues entailed—the quality and artistic status of this repertory, especially in comparison to Beethoven's 'heroic' and other canonical works; and the criteria for judging that status—have been largely ignored. Hepokoski too ignores them, unless the very fact of his discussing the overture to *Die Ruinen von Athen* were taken as implying a belief that it is comparable to the masterworks with which he associates it. (He rejects on speculative grounds the possibility "that the overture's structure and content were (...) randomly or casually assembled," without noting that in fact considerable sketching survives for it.[12]) In fact, however, this overture (I say nothing about the remainder of the work) is one of Beethoven's least successful movements, arguably on the same unhappy level as *Der glorreiche Augenblick* and the choruses for dramas by Treitschke and Kotzebue, and well below *Wellingtons Sieg* or the *König Stephan* and *Namensfeier* overtures. The musical ideas lack character or quality, their motivic, rhythmic, and contrapuntal working-out is simplistic, and the orchestration adds little. It is difficult *not* to associate these deficiencies with the overture's underarticulated formal plan which, as Nicholas Mathew has argued with respect to other movements from this repertory, is too rudimentary (even if ambiguous) to foster useful hermeneutic activity.[13] *Formenlehre* must never forget that it is a work's aesthetic qualities that make us care about its form in the first place.

Response to the Comments

James Hepokoski

Response to William E. Caplin

William E. Caplin's comments on my essay "Sonata Theory and Dialogic Form" reaffirm his belief in the priority of 'formal functions' over 'formal types.' His discussions of the three overtures in question, though—particularly that of *Idomeneo*—fail to demonstrate the persuasiveness of such a style of analysis. Instead, they can suggest the opposite: the pitfalls of relying exclusively on the form-functional method. The larger issue in play here is not that method's particularities, which can often be very helpful. Rather, it is that within any method it is inadvisable to pursue formal analysis by extracting an individual work out of an established tradition of craft and its expectations, then reading its surface structures in the abstract, liberated from the social and historical influences on its construction and implied genre. Hard cases, then—as one finds in some of these works—can tempt one to pin our hopes only on "a certain 'artistic freedom' in (...) choice of formal type," as Caplin puts it, "as corny as it may sound" [>94].

Conceiving form dialogically helps to frame such issues more appropriately and to alleviate some of these risks. As a starting-point and sustaining handrail for nuanced analysis, it informs us, for instance, what we can reasonably expect to find within Austro-Germanic overtures (even odd or deformational ones) in the 1780-1812 period; what their available formal options and their deformational limits were; what kinds of structural choices were by and large inconceivable within those limits; and therefore what kinds of readings it is inappropriate to produce. My discussions of these overtures did not seek to declare 'what form they were in,' nor did they claim to solve or downplay the structural problems that those pieces presented to us. Rather, they posed the issue thus: given our understanding of how overtures were almost invariably manufactured during this period (what their construction-options actually were), what happens when we read formally anomalous overtures through the dialogical lenses of those generic norms? And might it not be reasonable to suppose that these norms were the ones most likely to have been operative for the initial production and reception of such overtures, at least among informed composers and listeners—in whose minds, in part, the perception of the 'form' could thereby be concretized into a meaningful whole?

Little need be said about Caplin's *Egmont* reply. I do not dispute his observation that the 'loose' and 'tight-knit' organization of P and S in both the exposition and recapitulation might be regarded as reversed from the high-classical norm (or at least from what I would call the first-level-default choices for P- and S-construction), although I would not place the analytical weight on this observation that Caplin does, particularly because within sonata-form practice there are so many different P- and S-theme types, both loose and tight-knit, within the generic system of sonata-compositional options.[1] Still, it would appear that our two views of this overture are at least compatible, if different in emphasis and implication.

This cannot be said of his discussions of the other two overtures. When considered with the concerns of dialogic form in mind, Caplin's reading of the overture to *Idomeneo* is indefensible: our two understandings of the piece could not be more dissimilar. His analysis starts from the accurate observation that the piece does not feature what both of us would regard as a fully unfurled or (in his words) "genuine development section" [>92]. Rather, mm. 82-92 are more retransitional, something that he acknowledges that I also pointed out in my own essay. (I had mentioned "a brief, essentially retransitional developmental space" [>75], which within Sonata-Theory terminology amounts to the same thing: a development proper is replaced by material that in this context functions more as a retransition—here somewhat extended.) This is only to say that *Idomeneo* is still interpretable as unfolding in a dialogue with the concept of 'sonata form' but in this case might be situated (as Caplin notes) within our category of the common Type 1 sonata ('sonata without development').[2]

It is curious that to make this point Caplin refers to 'the overture genre,' since in the remainder of his *Idomeneo* discussion he proceeds as if unaware that in overtures (unlike in the first movements of many, even most multimovement works of the time) the exposition is never repeated.[3] This oversight triggers an intensifying series of improbable assertions: that in this case alone (1), Mozart set out to suggest the presence of a non-normative expositional repeat (2), following a clearly articulated final caesura [m. 82] obviously closing off the exposition proper (3), and eleven full bars of retransition based on P-material (4), and that he then proceeded to treat that nongeneric repeat deformationally (5) by eliding it, shortly into the transition (6), with an aborted development (7), which then itself, soon enervated, collapses "mid-stream (...) much before having even arrived at the recapitulation" (8). Even more curiously, as I noted in my original essay, in *Classical Form* Caplin himself had discussed a model-type that must surely have been the more relevant dialogical precedent at hand, that of the sonata (often interpretable as a Type 1) with truncated recapitulation.

Caplin complements this confusion with the unlikely assertion that the secondary theme of *Idomeneo* begins in m. 35.[4] Such a conclusion is the product of a set of three interlocking convictions that Sonata Theory does not share. First, because of his initial definitions, he does not acknowledge the possibility of the not uncommonly occurring V:PAC MC that can precede what is far more intuitively the launching of S.[5] Second, he clings to the outdated conviction that all expositions must contain a subordinate theme (a concept now reconfigured as a 'subordinate-theme *function*'). Third, and consequently, whenever he encounters a work with what amounts to a V:PAC MC, like this one,[6] he must treat it, by prior definition, as the 'end' of at least one part of a 'subordinate-theme function' and proceed to search out some earlier module that he can try to identify as such. For all of Caplin's qualifications in *Classical Form*, it would seem that the rule for locating subordinate themes in a major-mode work is simply a matter of finding the first mid-expositional V:PAC (or, in a minor-mode work, the first III:PAC or v:PAC), then backtracking to find something that one can claim as beginning that 'function,' no matter how counterintuitive that claim might be.

Caplin's reading of the overture to *Die Ruinen von Athen* is somewhat more defensible: he construes it as a 'large ternary' form featuring a (subdominant) 'interior theme,' following his discussion of these structures and terms in *Classical Form*, pp. 211-16, where they appear under a discussion of 'slow-movement forms.'[7] Now, to be sure, if one considers only the *Allegro, ma non troppo* (mm. 29ff) of the overture, it is possible to observe resemblances between Caplin's general descriptions and portions of this overture.[8] It is also clear that in this case the extremely unusual (in 1811-12 almost unthinkable), quasi-episodic rounded-binary 'interior theme' in the subdominant, mm. 61-92, adds plausibility to this reading.

All this is fine so far as it goes. Nonetheless, there are obstacles to adopting this view as sufficient. Historically considered, a 'large ternary' format, for example—whose ABA' shape was always a viable option within slow movements, which did not limit themselves to sonata realizations—is normatively (perhaps invariably?) a self-standing structure, without an extended introduction. Here, though, we do have a slow introduction, one whose presence conditions our perception of the likely format-at-hand in ways to which I shall return. And even if we believe that this is not a problem for analytical interpretation—that any form could be selected for any overture—we are still left with the issue of *why* Beethoven, in this overture alone, decided to override all standard practices with regard to the overture-construction of his day. In other words, what Caplin factors out of his analysis is the concept of dialogic form itself—the idea that compositional forms do not appear at random or in arbitrary, *ad hoc* contexts but rather in dialogue with the gravitational pulls of standardized formats and practices, even when those dialogues are notably deformational (as often happens with quasi-illustrative or dramatic overtures). Without any grasp of dialogic form, it is certainly possible to agree with Caplin's reading. But the whole point of the dialogic concept is not to read 'apparent' (or puzzling) structures as singularities in the abstract, however much they might seem to conform to central features of current definitions. Those apparent similarities may only be fortuitous secondary effects of other, more compelling structural purposes. Fixing our attentions only on those similarities can blind us to the ways in which the composer may have set the piece into dialogue with the in-place generic norms and expectations of his or her own day.

As I noted, the immediate historical context of the overture to *Die Ruinen von Athen* is one in which, in 1811-12, there were only two viable generic options for the construction of overtures. The first, and overwhelmingly the most common (especially in the Mozart-Beethoven tradition), was sonata form, in overtures always deployed without an expositional repeat, and with or without an optional slow introduction preceding the sonata proper.[9] The second, far more infrequently selected option (perhaps more French-inflected in its day) was the freer, potpourri overture. The generic/analytical problem with this overture is that it provides conflicting generic signals. In his reply Caplin reduces its sonata aspects to "a main theme and a (highly condensed) development" [>93]. That is too short a list. Strong, virtually unmistakable sonata-genre signals are provided here by four prominent passages: (1) the extended slow introduction itself, in Beethoven (and others) strongly predictive of a sonata-form-to-come, especially when that prediction is followed by the forward-vectored launching of an *Allegro*; (2) the character of the first theme of the *Allegro, ma non troppo*, readily understandable as a 'standard' P-theme type, thus reinforcing the expectation aroused by the introduction; (3) the presence of a recognizable, if brief, developmental space, with the typically developmental, sequential workings of P; this is no mere retransition; (4) the beginning of a clear, tonic reprise of P following this generically clear development. The counter-sonata features, of course (beyond the absence of a clear TR), concern what we initially expect to be S-space: instead of anything normative, we encounter the wrong key, the wrong form, and so on, in the presumed exposition, making this passage seem indeed, as Caplin correctly notes, like an 'interior theme;' and this theme is completely excised from the presumed recapitulation, in which Beethoven abruptly extinguishes the overture at the end of P.

The strongest analyses of such a work need to begin by confronting the conflicted problematics of this odd concatenation of signals, not by simplifying those matters by adducing contextually neutralized formats bolstered, in the end, with the assertion that Beethoven must simply have been exerting "a certain 'artistic freedom'" [>94] that completely—

and only in this work—sidelined the grand tradition of classical-overture construction. This is not an overture to be 'solved' in any declarative manner. Rather, like many others, this is a startlingly non-normative piece whose considerable challenges and generic ambiguities ask instead to be patiently explicated, then brought further into the realm of hermeneutic interpretation—the 'why' question, which should be the ultimate goal of all analyses.[10]

Response to James Webster

In large part Warren Darcy and I devised Sonata Theory during the past two decades as a consequence of our growing awareness of the shortcomings of the dominant English-language styles of analytical commentary. These were then-entrenched orthodoxies that we had learned thoroughly, taught, and passed on for years. In time and upon deeper reflection, we became convinced that such arguments and approaches, however influential and for all of their much-welcome benefits over earlier methods, were marred by recurring blind spots, doctrinal overemphases, and questionable assumptions. Some of these (like Cone's overdrawn version of the 'sonata principle') were regularly repeated, and are sometimes still averred today, as normalized tenets of the analytical faith. All too often, these modes of inquiry had not thought through the issues deeply enough, stopping short of addressing more complete and productive questions of form, including such matters as recapitulatory 'resolution' and the relation between historically produced musical structures and a responsible, critical hermeneutics.

Both in his original essay and in his reply to mine, James Webster deploys a pattern of argument that is characteristic of a style of analysis that we found insufficient. He takes a musical discussion or problematic issue only so far, then stops short, terminating further inquiry with a confident pronouncement. One is satisfied too quickly, at too low a level of consideration. My concern with regard to Webster's treatment of the *Jupiter* symphony, for instance,[11] was not that his tabulated list of data was unhelpful, but rather that once it had been produced he assessed the structural issue to be solved and shut down the process of analysis and interpretation almost before it had begun. Similarly, in the first part of his reply to my essay, he is content (with regard to the *Egmont* issue) only to recite familiar—and from our point of view, problematic—orthodoxies about recapitulatory fifth-relations and unusual key-relations in the nineteenth century. And in the final part of his reply, Webster avoids confronting the curious (and difficult) *Die Ruinen von Athen* problem by washing his hands of it, declaring the overture to be aesthetically lacking, "one of Beethoven's least successful movements," charged with "deficiencies" that he suggests are all too readily associated with the piece's "underarticulated formal plan" [>100]. End of discussion: the overture is not worth the trouble of being commented upon.[12] But the *raison d'être* of Sonata Theory is not to promote an aesthetic assessment as a badge of the analyst's taste; rather, it is to advance the dialogical understanding of a musical discourse—*any* musical discourse that one chooses—within history.

Still, I am pleased that he chose to resuscitate the traditional view regarding recapitulatory fifth-relation and what "counts" as a resolution [>96], in part because it was once such a common conviction among certain schools of analysis but also in part because it is so easily amended through a more careful thinking through the issue. What is striking at the outset is that the very assertions (and often the very examples) that Webster brings up are ones that Darcy and I have already addressed head-on in earlier writings (including ones directly cited in his response).[13] Rather then addressing our published reasons for finding the 'fifth-relation' claim to be insufficient, Webster reverts to an earlier status of the assertion, remaining content only to restate the original position.[14] Readers interested in following our reasoning more closely and in a broader context may be referred to the passages cited in note 13. For the present, I shall summarize only a few points in response to Webster's assertions.

The first and most important crossroad to face is the question of how to interpret the tonal implications for 'resolution' in such a work as the *Egmont* overture, whose exposition moves from F minor to A-flat major (i–III), but whose recapitulation traverses the keys of F minor and D-flat major (i–VI). Thus, the overture's S is never sounded in the tonic (i or I), even while it is obvious that the recapitulatory S-material in VI replicates that of the exposition a fifth lower. Webster wants this to "count," unproblematically, as a resolution, since "a recapitulation at the fifth below remains an effective procedure of tonal 'grounding'" (and hence he does "not believe that this tonal disposition *as such* 'demands' interpretation") [>99].[15] In other words, within this situation, whether S appears in the tonic or not does not matter. *Pari passu*, the implication must be that it did not matter to Beethoven, who might just as well, we suppose, have placed the S-theme in the tonic F major, since in terms of a satisfactory "grounding" this would have produced no "effective" difference. At least from the standpoint of Sonata Theory, Webster prefers not to recognize the essential problem, thereby walling himself off from an inquiry into the most provocative tonal feature of the piece and its expressive (and programmatic) implications. It may be helpful to back up and define our terms more clearly.

First, *Egmont*'s S in VI certainly "counts" as being a constituent of the recapitulation (or recapitulatory space) [>96], since that space, in the view of Sonata Theory, is defined by the disposition of its (rotationally determined) thematic contents, not exclusively by its tonal normativity or non-normativity. Webster's suggestion that we think that the restoration of an S-theme (or part thereof) in a nontonic area is "not 'really' recapitulated" (an imagined position that he then decries as "an (absurd) result") is inaccurate [>97]. Such an S-theme (or module[s] thereof) is of course "'really' recapitulated"—tracked through in full in the recapitulatory space—even if it is never sounded ("resolved") in the tonic. But it matters whether or not an S-theme (or part thereof) appears in the tonic. Surely a theme can be "'really' recapitulated" but not tonally resolved.

But why cannot a 'fifth-relation'—sounding a theme in VI in the recapitulation that was originally heard in III (whether it eventually returns to the tonic or not, as Webster notes often happens)—really "count" as a fully satisfactory ("effective") resolution? Isn't VI good enough? After all, "[t]ransposition down a fifth indeed creates a powerful analogy to the V→I relation of the sonata principle" [>97]. This point is obvious and in our own discussions of these cases we have underscored the same observation. But still, VI is not I. Above all, they are dissimilar in terms of tonal "resolution" (a concept that we construe dialogically according to the generic norm within sonata-practice), notwithstanding the self-evident analogy of III→VI to the V→I norm in major-mode sonatas. This is not a difficult dilemma to steer through. The tonal 'analogy' is of course still there—which accounts for why VI is so often found in such cases—but the generically commonplace fifth-relation in this case 'misfires' (is it being adduced as a 'too-automatic' gesture within the generic system?), driving the S-theme or portion thereof into a nonresolving key. On the basis of generic experience it is most analytically responsible to conclude that we are to observe and register this tonal misfiring as significant. In doing so, one should acknowledge the analogy with the V→I norm. But one should also acknowledge that the resulting VI, in these cases (or even in Cone's vague "closer relation with the tonic" [quoted by Webster >97]), is not I, even though the music might soon enough 'correct itself' *en route* back into the tonic. However trenchant it might be, analogy is not the same as identity, nor is it even "effective" identity. (Indeed, the distinction between analogy and identity is the central point of analytical and hermeneutic interest.) And 'tonal resolution,' historically, generically, and dialogically considered, is about the successful attaining of tonal 'identity,' in this case within recapitulatory space.

Apart from the above considerations, the traditional fifth-relation argument does not consider that the V→I relation applies primarily to *major-mode* sonatas. In the majority of minor-mode sonatas, where the most common norm was to move from i to III in the exposition (as in the *Egmont* Overture), the expected recapitulatory resolution was a III→I relation, not a V→I relation.[16] Why would a V→I relation be *ipso facto* an "effective" tonal grounding in this case? Why should we assume that in suggesting a tonal relation typical of *major*-mode sonatas, a *minor*-mode one is thereby tonally grounded to the point where our curiosity is now fully satisfied, discouraging the need for any further questioning, much less 'interpretation'? This line of analytical commentary brushes aside provocative generic issues at the very point where they start to become interesting.

Finally, one should note that the same model of attenuated discussion may be observed in Webster's citations of the expanded key relationships often found in Schubert (for example, the String Quintet) and Brahms (the Third Symphony). In brief, summarizing here our differing interpretation, for instance, of the Schubert situation: when portions of S (or a trimodular block) appear out-of-tonic in the recapitulation—usually at S's onset, as a result of fifth-transposition and on the way to the attainment of an eventual tonic down the road—we do not merely declare that because those modules are "'constituents' of the form," they must "count" as "effective" tonal resolutions [>96]. Instead, we have written that "they signify a *tonal alienation* of [that] portion of S, demonstrating that certain features of post-MC space are forever nonassimilable into the tonic. They remain irrecoverably alienated from tonal resolution. Tonal alienation of this sort may be found in many of Schubert's pieces."[17] (It is also found in those of several other composers, especially, as Webster notes, as one proceeds into later decades of the nineteenth century.) In circumstances such as those found in the first movement of the Schubert Quintet we have both a *full* recapitulation and a *resolving* recapitulation, even while significant parts of S's opening, for whatever reason, are not permitted to participate in the larger generic *telos* of tonic-key, tonal resolution.

Observing the matter from this perspective opens the door to broader, more unsettling hermeneutic problems of implied structure and historically informed content. What might it mean that Beethoven, Schubert, Brahms, or anyone else decided to keep this or that portion of S (or all of S) forever out-of-tonic? Sonata Theory starts with a conviction that, for us as analysts, such things ought to mean something, not nothing. In trying to unpack the problematics of any piece's individuality, we try to steer clear of ready-made answers. Analytical inquiries, in whatever system or methodology, should open up problematic features of works, not shut them down.

Notes

SONATA THEORY AND DIALOGIC FORM

James Hepokoski

1. The method is laid out in James Hepokoski & Warren Darcy, *Elements of Sonata Theory: Norms, Types, and Deformations in the Late-Eighteenth-Century Sonata* (2006).

2. Mark Evan Bonds, "The Paradox of Musical Form," Chapter 1 of *Wordless Rhetoric: Musical Form and the Metaphor of the Oration* (1991), pp. 13–52.

3. A third, more recent category is William E. Caplin's 'functional' theory of form (*Classical Form: A Theory of Formal Functions for the Instrumental Music of Haydn, Mozart, and Beethoven* (1998)). In this method thematic and intrathematic units are considered primarily in terms of their musical functions on their way to essential form-defining cadential goals—such functions as successions of beginnings (initiatory units), middles (continuations), and endings (cadences). (Other functions, such as framing functions, are also part of the process.) Sonata Theory is also a system attentive to local functions and purposes—beginnings, middles, endings, cadential goals, and so on. It differs from form-functional theory in some of its basic definitions (and hence in its terminology and ramifications), in its concern for what it regards as the more fundamental concepts around which the sonata process turns, and in its insistence on proceeding beyond the identification of functions into larger questions of historical dialogue and expressive hermeneutics. Accepting certain aspects of thematic function as self-evident, Sonata Theory invites one into an expansive, interpretive way of thinking about sonata procedures as realized in individual works.

4. James Hepokoski, "Back and Forth from *Egmont*: Beethoven, Mozart, and the Nonresolving Recapitulation" (2001), pp. 127–54.

5. Exceptions, nuances, and caveats abound, of course: the topic is extremely complex. See James Hepokoski, "Beyond the Sonata Principle" (2002), 91–154.

6. 'Sonata-space' is that space occupied by the exposition, development, and recapitulation (whose ending is identified as that moment corresponding rhetorically and thematically with the conclusion of the exposition). Introductions and codas are regarded as accretions articulated outside of sonata-space. See, e.g., *Elements of Sonata Theory*, pp. 281–83.

7. *Elements of Sonata Theory*, pp. 170–77.

8. What immediately follows the overture is Ilia's recitative *Quando avran fine omai* (which begins on G minor), and this leads to the G-minor aria (No. 1) *Padre, germani, addio!*

9. On the truncated recapitulation see *Elements of Sonata Theory*, pp. 247–49 and Caplin, *Classical Form*, p. 216 (where it is included in the chapter "Slow-Movement Forms"). On the important question of tempo in this instance, see note 24 below and the accompanying discussion in the text [>84-85].

10. This passage is mentioned as an example—along with others—of the blocked MC in *Elements of Sonata Theory*, p. 47.

11. *Elements of Sonata Theory*, p. 29. From a different point of view, form-function theory grants a TR function (and hence a TR designation) only to those spans that conclude with a half cadence or dominant arrival in either the tonic or the new key (Caplin, *Classical Form*, pp. 133-38). If that span ends with a I:PAC it retains P-function; if with a V:PAC it fulfills an S-function (pp. 97, 111–19, 201–03). As opposed to this—and for a host of reasons that would require a separate, extended discussion to deal with here—Sonata Theory recognizes that a TR leading ultimately to an S-zone may indeed conclude with either a V:PAC MC or (much more rarely) a I:PAC MC as third- and fourth-level defaults (*Elements of Sonata Theory*, pp. 25–40). In the case of *Die Ruinen von Athen*, however, it is also possible to suggest that Beethoven might have—for whatever reason—omitted the transition-zone completely.

12. *Elements of Sonata Theory*, p. 275, notes the example of the finale to Schubert's Piano Quintet in A, D. 667 (*Trout*) along with that of the B-flat Quartet, D. 36.

13. While not downplaying the strangeness of this 'wrong-key' subdominant move in the overture, it might be worth remarking that in subsequent works ('late Beethoven'), we often find a strong—and unusual—subdominant emphasis: descending-third chains, the fugal answer in Op. 131/i, and so on. Beethoven's subdominant leanings in the late style have not gone unremarked, and in some instances such subdominants have been provided with a hermeneutic or representational function (beyond, that is, their typical pastoral or plagal resonances). See, e.g., Michael Spitzer, *Music as Philosophy: Adorno and Beethoven's Late Style* (2006), p. 77: "Chord IV thus becomes a token of the irrational or the archaic, which is why it exerts such a strong gravitational pull on late works like the mass. As Lodes argues, in the mass the subdominant, often allied with modality (e.g., the Mixolydian), is a symbol for the Deity or the Absolute (see also Kinderman 1985)." The first reference is to Birgit Lodes, "'When I try, now and then, to give musical form to my turbulent feelings': The Human and the Divine in the Gloria of Beethoven's *Missa solemnis*" (1998), pp. 143–79. The second is to William Kinderman, "Beethoven's Symbol for the Deity in the *Missa Solemnis* and the Ninth Symphony" (1985), pp. 102–18. See also William Drabkin, *Beethoven: Missa Solemnis* (1991), p. 22: "One of Beethoven's commonest harmonic procedures in the *Missa Solemnis* is to emphasize the subdominant. (...) Moreover, the blatantly anti-tonal flattened VII—the subdominant of the subdominant—becomes a part of Beethoven's harmonic vocabulary". Also of interest is Robert S. Hatten's general characterization of the subdominant (as an example of 'markedness of key relations') in *Musical Meaning in Beethoven: Markedness, Correlation, and Interpretation* (1994), p. 43: "The [tonal] move to the subdominant [as opposed to the dominant] (...) is backward-directed, static, stable, and closural."

14. Caplin, *Classical Form*, pp. 97–123; *Elements of Sonata Theory*, pp. 124-31, 139–40. Caplin observes, in particular, that this rounded binary format (his 'small ternary form') is almost never found at the basis of secondary themes in the normative classical repertory in the decades before, say, 1820: "A major exception pertains to the small ternary form, as the three functions of exposition,

contrasting middle, and recapitulation [reprise], rarely appear in a subordinate theme" (p. 97; see also the accompanying and explanatory p. 270, note 9, which remarks on the presence of many such rounded, lyrically enclosed S themes in the works of later ('romantic') composers). When such rounded themes are found in the expositions of later composers, they typically give the impression of an inset, textless song or self-contained, closed lyrical effusion called upon to occupy one or more of the thematic zones of a sonata form.

15. Thus quotations in the overture to *Die Ruinen von Athen* from the subsequent incidental music occur only as the constituent elements of the bipartite introduction to the overture; the sonata-deformation music (*Allegro, ma non troppo*) does not contain overt quotations. Some of the P-theme of the overture might (obliquely) suggest a flickering of string-figuration near the opening of the recitative before No. 7 *Mit reger Freude, die nie erkaltet* ("With lovely joy that never cools").

16. Suzanne Steinbeck, *Die Ouvertüre in der Zeit von Beethoven bis Wagner: Probleme und Lösungen* (1973), for example—a study concerned overwhelmingly with sonata-form constructions and their variants, along with their potential for programmatic considerations—suggests that the only significant alternative to sonata-grounded overtures in the early nineteenth century was that of the non-sonata-like '*Reihungsprinzip*' or '*das Prinzip der Aneinanderreihung*' (p. 114), that is, the succession of closed, discrete sections, usually prolepses of the opera-to-come, of what we call here the potpourri overture, all indicative of a process of the 'dissolution of sonata form' ('*Auflösung der Sonatensatzform*,' p. 112).

17. *Le Jeune Henri* is typically cited as a predecessor to Rossini's potpourri overture to *Guillaume Tell* (1829), while several of Boieldieu's operatic overtures, at least from the 1810s and 1820s, are sometimes seen as decisive spurs in the direction of the potpourri or medley overture for lighter works in subsequent decades. Spontini's overture to *La Vestale* (1807) was famously cited—and criticized—by Wagner in 1841 ("Über die Ouvertüre") for, in effect (and "in a certain sense"), beginning "the history of this *potpourri* [overture]," although on closer inspection that overture is better regarded as a slow introduction leading to a loose sonata form whose recapitulatory space, following the reinstating of P, proceeds to heroic, coda-like variants of aspects of TR and S, themselves closely related to P-ideas.

The subject of European overture formatting beyond sonata norms (or even within them) in the 1770-1830 period needs further investigation. Basil Deane, "The French Operatic Overture from Grétry to Berlioz" (1972-1973), pp. 67–80, provides an enticing overview of some of the issues in play—though most notably about the French approach to the sonata-form overture, which was considerably looser, freer, than the Austro-Germanic approach: "The experimentation with harmony and thematic material led to an overall freedom of formal structure. (...) This is particularly apparent in the treatment of the recapitulation. Here the order of subjects is often reversed [presumably Sonata Theory's Type 2 sonata?], or the whole recapitulation may be greatly altered, condensed, or dropped in favour of an important coda" (p. 76). In touching on the overture to *La Vestale*—and apparently accepting Wagner's inaccurate assessment of its form—Deane did claim, however, that it "accentuated the prevailing trend towards the *pot-pourri* overture" (p. 79).

18. Interestingly enough, at least rudimentary sonata-oriented claims have been made recently for *Wellingtons Sieg* by Stephen Rumph, *Beethoven after Napoleon: Political Romanticism in the Late Works* (2004), pp. 175–81.

19. *Elements of Sonata Theory*, pp. 205–12, 217.

20. The incidental music from *Die Ruinen von Athen* was revived (recycled) in 1822 for the reopening of the Theater in der Josefstadt to serve as the incidental music for *Die Weihe des Hauses*. This included slightly altered versions of most of the numbers of the incidental music of *Die Ruinen von Athen* (including the Chorus of Dervishes, the Turkish March, etc.), with the original text only slightly altered and 'pointed' toward Austria and the Emperor Franz by Carl Meisl (who also wrote the new play, *Die Weihe des Hauses* (*The Consecration of the House*)). At that time Beethoven decided to insert one additional chorus ('new' to the 1810s, WoO 98) and to compose an entirely new overture.

21. Cf. note 16 above (Steinbeck, 1973). While the assessment of *Die Ruinen von Athen* as a rondo or rondo variant is so *outré* as hardly to require comment, it may be instructive to pause to remind ourselves of why this is so, for the reasoning process involved helps to illustrate by negative example the larger concept of dialogic form. As is widely known, rondos were typically deployed in finales (especially in concertos), in some slow movements, and in a handful of solo keyboard or solo-instrument (with accompaniment) works. Were one to find an overture (or a fast-tempo first movement) in an unequivocal rondo or sonata-rondo format, that would be so strikingly counter-normative that it would immediately lead to the question of why such an unusual choice was made—and interpretive justifications for it would have to be proposed: it would by no means be a 'neutral' or purely 'abstract' choice. To find a deformational rondo (as opposed to a typical or obvious one) would be even more counter-normative.

More specifically, to regard the *allegro, ma non troppo* portion of this overture as a rondo, one would have to regard 'P^1' (m. 29), or even P^1+P^2, as the rondo theme. But that theme features none of the earmark rondo-theme characteristics typical of the period—indeed, it unfolds very much like a typical P-theme within a sonata movement—and it recurs only once more in the piece, at the recapitulatory moment, m. 129. In other words the overture to *Die Ruinen von Athen* is not arrayed in any typical fast-tempo rondo format of the period, unless one wishes to revert to the idea that every 'ternary' format (ABA'—if that is one's reading of the overture in question here) is also a rudimentary rondo form (a 'first rondo form' [or Marx's once-proposed category of 'second rondo form,' with only one episode or *Seitensatz*]; cf. Caplin, *Classical Form*, p. 284, note 1). Additionally, one would have to accept the concept of an *allegro*-tempo 'first rondo form' (in this period) *preceded by an expansive, slow introduction*—at best an extremely rare, probably nonexistent practice, particularly within orchestral works. Finally, were one still trying to keep the rondo-option inadvisably alive, doubtless because of the precipitous drop into IV at m. 61, along with the rounded-binary shape of what follows, one might imagine a claim that a refrain-statement might have been suppressed in this overture, in the manner, perhaps, of the AB–C–A format of the finale of Mozart's Piano Sonata in B-flat, K. 570, iii. (In such a reading in the overture, mm. 61–92 would serve as B, the developmental space as C.) But the differences between that finale (discussed as a variant of the five-part rondo, AB–AC–A, in *Elements of Sonata Theory*, pp. 400–01) and *Die Ruinen von Athen* are so obvious that they need not be belabored here. The larger point is that the five-part rondo variant is a structure that juxtaposes different 'closed melodic sections,' which is just what happens in K. 570, iii; 'developments' (a signal of sonata or sonata-rondo procedure) play no part in it. And, conversely, no variant of the Type 4 sonata ('fully fledged sonata-rondo') that has yet surfaced to our attention brings back its recapitulatory refrain after a developmental space only to truncate the remainder of the recapitulation (see *Elements of Sonata Theory*, pp. 404–12).

22. Cf. note 13 above, citing Spitzer (2006), who associated some of late Beethoven's subdominant inflections with expressions of 'the irrational or the archaic.'

23. *Elements of Sonata Theory*, p. 249.

24. In his discussion of truncated recapitulations (*Classical Form*, pp. 216–17)—housed within Chapter 14, "Slow-Movement Forms"—Caplin observes that "such a truncated recapitulation (...) creates a form that resembles a large ternary, one whose interior theme has been replaced by a transition and subordinate theme. (...) Until the transition and subordinate theme are perceived to be eliminated from the recapitulation, the listener has every reason to believe that the movement is a regular sonata ([normally] without development)." In Table 14.1, Caplin includes, along with many of the works cited above, Mozart's Clarinet Quintet in A, K. 581, ii, Violin Sonata in F, K. 376/374d, ii, and Violin Sonata in B-flat, K. 378/316d, ii. – As has been noted by others as well, the truncated recapitulation also surfaces in a few slow movements of Brahms, such as those of the Second and Third Symphonies; see. e.g., Elaine Sisman, "Brahms's Slow Movements: Reinventing the 'Closed' Forms" (1990), pp. 79–104, which approaches the topic from a different perspective.

25. Another difference, of course, is the *Idomeneo* Overture's more full-throated entry into *bona-fide* TR-space in the truncated recapitulation before self-aborting via an extended recomposition, a feature not found in *Die Ruinen von Athen* or in most of the slow movements cited above.

COMMENTS ON JAMES HEPOKOSKI'S ESSAY "SONATA THEORY AND DIALOGIC FORM"

William E. Caplin

1. James Webster also cites Bonds in a similar connection in his essay "*Formenlehre* in Theory and Practice."

2. In that Hepokoski's (and Warren Darcy's) theory of musical form (see *Elements of Sonata Theory*) is based on largely the same repertory as my theory of formal functions, it is not surprising that we identify similar compositional processes taking place within these works. At the same time, we often con-

ceptualize what occurs in fundamentally different ways, which frequently yields quite varying formal analyses. In footnotes 3 and 9 of his essay [>111], Hepokoski alludes to some of these theoretical differences, which, unfortunately, limitations of space in this response prohibit me from entertaining. Readers who are interested in seeing how our differing perspectives further play out analytically may wish to read our respective essays in *Beethoven's* Tempest *Sonata: Perspectives of Analysis and Performance*, ed. Pieter Bergé (2009).

3. Telling, in this respect, is the fact that, with one exception, none of Hepokoski's analytical charts provide any phrase-structural readings of the various middle-ground formal regions (P, TR, S, etc.). Figure 2.2 indicates the 'trimodular block' at the basis of S, but no further phrase-structural details are shown.

4. Had Beethoven set the subordinate theme in the home-key major, the 'victorious' effect of the coda would have been entirely spoiled. Had he placed the theme in the home-key minor, the wonderful tonicization of the Neapolitan at m. 92 would have sounded pedestrian, lacking as it would the set-up that makes this harmony so magical in the exposition, namely, the modal shift from major to minor (m. 91). Setting the recapitulatory subordinate theme in D-flat major solves both of these problems and renders the appearance of the Neapolitan at m. 235 particularly fresh.

5. At best, one can identify at m. 43 a 'premature dominant arrival' (see *Classical Form*, p. 81).

6. See, e.g., Charles Rosen, *Sonata Forms*: "The form is (...) exceedingly common in opera overtures: excellent examples may be found in both *Idomeneo* and *The Marriage of Figaro* by Mozart, as well as in most of Rossini's overtures, Berlioz's *Waverly* overture, and elsewhere" (p. 107).

7. Hepokoski and Darcy identify this option, what they call a "type 3 sonata [regular sonata form] with expositional-repeat feint" (*Elements of Sonata Theory*, pp. 350–51), but reject it for overtures, citing the lack of expositional repeat for this genre.

8. My analytical reading of the exposition differs from Hepokoski's in that I hear the subordinate-theme group beginning at m. 35, where a new thematic process leads to perfect authentic cadential closure in the new key at m. 45.

9. On the definition of development function, including its most characteristic phrase-structural component, a 'core,' see *Classical Form*, Chapter 10.

10. Note that Hepokoski is silent on the phrase-structural organization of mm. 137ff.

11. The emphases on subdominant in late Beethoven cited by Hepokoski (note 13 [>112]) refer to vocal or fugal genres, not to any sonata-exposition contexts.

12. See *Classical Form*, pp. 212–14 ('interior theme' in 'large ternary'); pp. 233–34 (in 'five-part rondo'); p. 238 (in 'sonata-rondo'). See also Table 1.1 of my opening essay [>33].

13. *Classical Form*, p. 238.

14. Likewise, we could even identify an interior theme without necessarily invoking the large ternary form, though here I am making the case that this formal type is indeed the appropriate option for this overture.

COMMENTS ON JAMES HEPOKOSKI'S ESSAY "SONATA THEORY AND DIALOGIC FORM"

James Webster

1. Edward T. Cone, *Musical Form and Musical Performance* (1968), pp. 76–78 (the quotation on p. 77); Charles Rosen, *The Classical Style* (1971), pp. 72–74; *Sonata Forms* (1980), pp. 25, 272, 275–76; his formulation is that the material in the dominant creates a 'structural dissonance' that must be 'resolved.'; James Webster, "Sonata Form" (*The Revised New Grove Dictionary*, 2001), Vol. 23, pp. 688, 693–94, 696.

2. James Webster, "Schubert's Sonata Form and Brahms's First Maturity" (1977–78), pp. 33–35; (1978–79), pp. 64–65, 68. Of course Hepokoski knows this; see his "Back and Forth from *Egmont*" (2001), pp. 153–54.

3. Donald F. Tovey, "[Brahms:] Quartet in C Minor, Op. 60" (1901), pp. 209–10.

4. On the Brahms, see Peter H. Smith, *Expressive Forms in Brahms's Instrumental Music* (2005), pp. 47–49, 81–85, 206–10.

5. Susan McClary, "Identity and Difference in Brahms's Third Symphony" (1993), p. 340, discusses the D-major recapitulation of the second theme in hermeneutic terms, but not the D-minor closing group.

6. Ernst Oster, "The Dramatic Character of Beethoven's *Egmont* Overture" (1983), pp. 209–22.

7. In any case, both Hepokoski and Darcy's *Elements of Sonata Theory* and Hepokoski's critiques of the sonata principle include frequent references to late Beethoven and Schubert.

8. Hepokoski and Darcy are aware of this issue; see the justifications in *Elements of Sonata Theory*, pp. 10–12 and Appendix 2.

9. The same objection has been made against my 'multivalent' method. And in fact, my results could also be obtained by 'normal' methods, given a sufficiently attentive observer. Nevertheless, as I say regarding a non-congruity in the *Jupiter* that I hadn't noticed until I applied the method, "this is the kind of thing the multivalent method encourages one to see" [>134]. Obviously, Hepokoski has available the analogous argument in favor of 'dialogic' formal thinking.

10. Thus (for what it is worth) the majority of my analytical publications beginning with "Brahms's *Tragic Overture*: The Form of Tragedy" (1983) present various, in part generically differentiated, formal readings, and often conclude that *the* form is indeterminate; likewise most deal in whole or in part with hermeneutic aspects.

11. William Kinderman, *Beethoven* (1995), pp. 169–80; Nicholas Cook, "The Other Beethoven: Heroism, the Canon, and the Works of 1813–14" (2003), pp. 3–24; Stephen Rumph, *Beethoven after Napoleon: Political Romanticism in the Late Works* (2004); Nicholas Mathew, "History Under Erasure: *Wellingtons Sieg*, the Congress of Vienna, and the Ruination of Beethoven's Heroic Style," pp. 17–61.

12. Gustav Nottebohm, *Zweite Beethoveniana* (1887), pp. 138, 143; Douglas Johnson et al., *The Beethoven Sketchbooks* (1985), pp. 203, 532.

13. Nicholas Mathew, "Beethoven and his Others: Criticism, Difference, and the Composer's Many Voices" (2006), 169–82.

RESPONSE TO THE COMMENTS

James Hepokoski

1. *Elements of Sonata Theory*, pp. 69–71, 77–92, 124–47, provides an inventory of some of the more frequently encountered P- and S-types and structures. One need only observe here that an observation of mere 'tight-knittedness' or 'looseness,' while by no means completely irrelevant, does not exhaust the available options within P- or S-norms.

2. Most of the overtures that Caplin cites—especially *Figaro* and the Rossini overtures—are also mentioned, along with others, in *Elements of Sonata Theory*, "[Five] Sonata Types and the Type 1 Sonata," pp. 344, 345–52.

3. *Elements of Sonata Theory*, pp. 20–22 ("Repetition Schemes"), pp. 346, 351.

4. From our perspective, this claim is unsustainable. The new module set forth at m. 35 is directly in the center of an ongoing, energy-gaining passage with all the textural earmarks of a normative Mozartian transition. (It also recurs in m. 70, of course, as the continuation portion of the sentential TM^{3} that begins at m. 64. It may be worth mentioning that concluding an extended pre-EEC section [the end of S or a TMB] with a rhyming return to material from TR—"to complete that trajectory"—is discussed in *Elements of Sonata Theory*, p. 141. Caplin's claim, as I understand it, must be that the material of this module both begins and ends the subordinate-theme area, which, apart from all of the other cited considerations, strikes me as highly unlikely.) An additional signal of 'normative' TR-space here (mm. 23–45) is found in the characteristic bass motion mm. 37-41: its generic $\hat{4}$-$\sharp\hat{4}$-$\hat{5}$, in this instance locking onto V of A major, which Mozart then treats as a blocked medial caesura (see the following note) and, soon thereafter, directs into a shift of mode onto A minor (m. 45), deploying one standard (though connotatively 'negative') way of beginning S-space. (On $\hat{4}$-$\sharp\hat{4}$-$\hat{5}$, see *Elements of Sonata Theory*, pp. 30–31; on the minor-mode onset of S, see *Elements of Sonata Theory*, pp. 119, 141–42.)

5. An example of the 'blocked-caesura' variant of it occurs in mm. 41–45 of this overture, with a *piano* S emerging in A minor, after the telltale caesura-gap, in m. 45. On the blocked MC, see *Elements of Sonata Theory*, pp. 47–48, which discusses this passage in the *Idomeneo* overture.

6. See, however, the qualification in the previous note.

7. I am not suggesting that a form normatively found in slow movements will never be found in a fast-tempo movement. Indeed, in my original essay I made something of the same argument with regard to the format of the sonata with truncated recapitulation.

8. In my original essay I acknowledged the similarities that he also perceives, and I remarked on the possibility of this perception—the concept of "something of a hybrid between a sonata form and a ternary, ABA' form" and so on. See the discussion around my original note 24 [>115].

9. As also noted in my discussion above of *Idomeneo*, the format of the *allegro*-tempo sonata proper was normally a Type 3—with a developmental space of variable length. Alternatively, the sonata could be a Type 1—without development or with only a brief link connecting exposition to recapitulation.

10. Subsequent to the writing of my "Sonata Theory and Dialogic Form" essay, another published mention of the overture to *Die Ruinen von Athen* has come to my attention: that of Axel Schröter in his highly informative volume on *Musik zu den Schauspielen August von Kotzebues: Zur Bühnenpraxis während Goethes Leitung des Weimarer Hoftheaters* (2006). Although he does not discuss its form in detail, Schröter's view (pp. 218–19) is that the overture is "neither a potpourri (...) nor a teleological sonata movement" but rather, it seems, an *ad hoc* structure or *unicum* explicable only either within the context of the whole set of incidental music, retrospectively (and thus ultimately in the manner of an epilogue or dramatic *Nachspiel*), or through an appeal to extramusical considerations. With regard to the latter, and somewhat similarly to my own reading of the structure's implications, Schröter, informed by a knowledge of the play-to-come, also suggests a parallel with the concept of ruins: "The [overture] may also be understood as a musical translation of [one's] groping search in a world that lies about one in rubble [*Trümmern*], in which one needs to gain one's proper orientation gradually—and thus also as a pendant to the depicted landscape of ruins [*Ruinen-Landschaft*]."

11. For my discussion on Webster's analysis of Mozart's *Jupiter* Symphony, see later in this volume [>148–150].

12. The issue in any analysis of the overture is not one of reinforcing the aesthetics of yesterday's academy but one of an earnest engagement with compositional intention, particularly vis-à-vis the historical implications of the cultural and political work originally planned for the occasion of the premiere. These are implications toward which the puzzlingly unusual structure of the overture can be understood to make a contribution. When Webster writes, "Certainly no concept like 'dialogic form' is required to grasp the formal problematics of Beethoven's overture" [>99], it is hard not to regard this as an unintentionally revealing claim, since it would seem that he is unwilling to engage or sufficiently acknowledge those problematics, preferring instead to provide us with his verdict regarding the work's inferiority.

13. We laid out our general rejoinders to these beliefs in *Elements of Sonata Theory* (pp. 242–45, "The 'Sonata Principle': A Problematic Concept," "The Fallacies of 'Closer Relation' and a 'Resolving' Fifth-Transposition"). In addition, I elaborated upon the logic behind these matters in two complementary articles from 2005, "Beyond the Sonata Principle," pp. 115–18, and "Back and Forth from *Egmont*: Beethoven, Mozart, and the Nonresolving Recapitulation," pp. 130–32.

14. To be sure, Webster mentions in general terms that he found some of the critiques in "Beyond the Sonata Principle" to be "dubious or overargued" [>96]. But instead of identifying what those problems were, much less seeking to counter them, he only restates his own variant of the mid-century, Conian 'sonata-principle' claim. Nowhere does he address the specifics of our objections to that claim.

15. Here the undefined terms are "effective procedure" and "tonal grounding." What, in this case, does "effective" mean? Who is authorized to set the standard of what is sufficiently "effective" within a historical style? And what, precisely, is meant by "grounding," since for Webster it is clearly not the same thing as a resolution in the tonic (which by implication might then be understood as only one subset of a more general "grounding" concept)? Is a "grounding" in VI, whatever that might suggest, the same, in "effect," as a grounding in I? Why would this be so? At the least, one would have to concede that restoring an S originally in III only in VI was *non-normative* when Beethoven used it in the *Egmont* overture—in which case the non-normativity itself becomes an invitation to pursue a more thoughtful analysis.

16. This is of course not the case where a minor-mode sonata moves from i to v in the exposition, a tonal option that we classify as a second-level default. The ramifications of this i-v choice are considered in *Elements of Sonata Theory*, pp. 314–17.

17. *Elements of Sonata Theory*, pp. 277–78, with italics added here. See also the more expanded, general treatment of post-MC nonresolution and its implications within recapitulatory spaces in "Back and Forth from *Egmont*" (2001), especially pp. 143–44, 151–53.

PART III
James Webster

&

THE CONCEPT OF MULTIVALENT ANALYSIS

Formenlehre in Theory and Practice

James Webster

During the second half of the twentieth century, theories of musical form were by and large considered *passé* in English-speaking countries, whether by Schenkerians (especially orthodox Schenkerians), who believed that they had overcome bad old analytical and theoretical traditions; or by postmodern writers, who tend to disdain analysis of 'the music itself' altogether. With the revival of interest in Tovey and other older writers, however, and the publication of such major contributions as Charles J. Smith's "Musical Form and Fundamental Structure: An investigation of Schenker's *Formenlehre*" (1996), William E. Caplin's *Classical Form* (1998), and James Hepokoski's and Warren Darcy's *Elements of Sonata Theory* (2006) signs of a rehabilitation of *Formenlehre* would seem to be present—even in the USA.

I shall begin by briefly discussing two important general issues affecting musical form. One is its double aspect: form as structure, and form in time. The other is the relation between form in general (or 'theory'), and the particular forms of individual works (or 'practice'). As we shall see, these two issues are closely related to each other, in ways that are particularly relevant to *Formenlehre*.

The double aspect of musical form arises from the fact that music takes place only in time; and yet a work or movement is also organized as a whole, as a structure. An old but still useful way of referring to this distinction is that of Kurt Westphal, who in the 1930s distinguished between '*Form*' and '*Formung*': between form-as-shape (balance, symmetry, proportions, architecture), and form-as-process (the dynamic development of musical ideas through time).[1] An analogous distinction to that between '*Form*' and '*Formung*' was proposed by Edward T. Cone; he distinguished in our reception of musical works between 'synoptic comprehension' (unity, structure, and so forth), and 'immediate apprehension'—"the mode by which we directly perceive the sensuous medium, its primitive elements, and their closest interrelationships."[2] Note that this formulation displaces the ostensibly immanent distinction between '*Form*' and '*Formung*' into the realm of psychology: between the subject's aesthetic contemplation of the work and his phenomenological experience of it.

Yet another related distinction, especially characteristic of Schenkerian thinking, is that between so-called outer and inner form: between, on the one hand, the construction of the work, or its 'surface design' (as one says), into so-and-so many sections having such-and-such relations to each other, and/or according to the successions of musical ideas; and, on the other hand, its organic or 'deep' structure, 'underneath' the surface (again, as one says), which develops in time according to its own logic, and bears no necessary correlation with the surface thematic events or even sectional divisions. (Note the ambiguity of the term 'structure' in these contexts; it can equally well connote the surface design of a work—its construction—and a 'deep' organization that is independent of the surface.)

Obviously, each of these dichotomies is framed as a binary opposition: '*Form*' vs. '*Formung*;' form as structure vs. form in time; surface design vs. organic deep structure; synoptic comprehension vs. immediate apprehension; and so forth. Indeed if we state only the first term in each pair, we shall obtain a good working definition of *Formenlehre*: form as structure; as shape; as design; defined by events on the musical surface; emphasizing the construction of the several parts and their relation to the whole; a matter of synoptic comprehension and aesthetic contemplation. Moreover, as everyone knows, such binary oppositions are usually associated with an asymmetrical value-relation, in which one pole is privileged at the expense of the other, and this asymmetry governs or shapes the discourse in question—often unconsciously. However, in the history of *Formenlehre* these oppositions have not been univalent. In music history and traditional pedagogy, '*Form*' has usually been privileged over '*Formung*,' comprehension over apprehension. Like many others, I therefore often feel it necessary to warn against the dangers, as for example in my article on sonata form in the *Revised New Grove Dictionary*: "Each movement grows bar by bar and phrase by phrase, with the meaning of each event depending both on its function in the structure and its dramatic context; its true form becomes clear only on close analysis in terms of its effect in performance."[3] For most Schenkerians, on the other hand, 'inner' form and 'structure' have been privileged over 'outer' form and 'design,' especially because of the close association between 'inner' form and notions of organicism.

I turn now to the issue of the general vs. the particular, or what Mark Evan Bonds has called the 'conformational' vs. the 'generative' aspects of form.[4] By necessity, *Formenlehre* (the theory or teaching of form) seeks to make valid generalizations about a large number of individual cases. The most obvious of these generalizations are 'the forms' themselves: binary form, da capo form, sonata form, rondo, and the rest. Generalization is equally important on the next-lower level, as it were, in the attempt to discriminate appropriately among the various different types within each of these large categories. Thus there is an enormous, if not always enlightening, literature on the various types and subtypes of binary form, of the da capo aria, and so forth. Regarding sonata form, recent discussions of this sort have tended to center on whether the term should be restricted to movements that more or less clearly exhibit *full* sonata form (exposition, elaborate development, full or nearly full recapitulation), with other formal types designated by different terms such as 'rounded binary' and 'sonata without development;'[5] or whether it should be understood in a maximally expansive sense that encompasses all the relevant formal types, the latter being understood as subtypes or options within it.[6] Ultimately these choices are more nearly matters of definition and categorization, and to some extent of analytical and critical style, than of 'objective' difference; what is essential, and unfortunately not always observed, is that one define one's terms and methods as clearly, and employ them as consistently, as possible.

In recent years the discussion of musical forms, at least in English, has moved away from understanding a given form as a fixed entity, defined more or less rigorously by particular features, towards two more flexible and more sophisticated concepts. One is the 'ideal type,' deriving from Max Weber, but introduced into musicology primarily by Carl Dahlhaus.[7] In the present context, this implies that the forms of individual movements should be analyzed according to their similarities and differences from a particular model or 'formal type' (which no actual movement exemplifies perfectly), in order to be able to compare them in a consistent manner; 'ideally,' the models themselves are generated in substantial part empirically and inductively. (In the context of formal analysis, 'type' is a special case of genre.) Indeed the term 'formal type' has become common in English; for example, the opening definition in my sonata-form article avoids the unqualified term 'form', reading instead: "The most important principle of form, or formal type, from the [later 18th century] well into the 20th."[8]

The other relevant concept is essentially a hermeneutic one, deriving from such figures as Gadamer, Jauss, and Iser, and representing a combination of reception theory, reader-response theory, and (again) genre theory, especially the so-called 'generic contract' of shared expectations between composer and listeners.[9] For example, if we settle in to listen to a symphony in late-18th-century style, we expect that if the opening movement is in a fast or moderately fast tempo, it will be in sonata form, and many particular kinds of events will occur within it; if these do not occur, we are surprised—pleasantly or unpleasantly, as the case may be. The form of a musical work has as much to do with convention, tradition, and context as with originality and particularity; a form is as much social as aesthetic in character. Nor are convention and listener-expectations constraining; on the contrary, it is their very existence that enabled the profound 'play,' on every level, of Haydn's instrumental music and Mozart's concertos and operas.

On a more 'practical' level of specificity are generalizations regarding specific features, or procedures, found in a particular form. Take for example the expressions 'first theme' and 'second theme.' In many German-language writings these terms are used as regulative concepts: a form is believed to be governed by the musical themes, the patterns of their occurrence and recurrence, and the nature of their development. That is, they become 'constituents' of the form, privileged over the remaining musical parameters. Even so sophisticated a writer as Dahlhaus was in the end an exponent of the 'thematicist' principle in music, with negative consequences for his analyses.[10] My impression is that many German-language writings on form still privilege the thematic domain.

In English, by contrast, ever since Tovey most writers have downgraded 'first theme' and 'second theme' to the level of 'mere' content or, in a semiotic mode, mere 'markers' of the tonal structure, the latter being taken as more fundamental. As governing concepts we prefer 'first group' and 'second group'; i.e., the music in the tonic and the music in the dominant. Particularly with respect to 18th-century music, where neither theory nor practice documents the necessity of a contrasting theme in the dominant, this view has become orthodoxy. Analogously, Schenker not only believed that 'true' musical form existed only in the background and deep middleground, but pronounced dogmatically that a sonata-form movement can be created only by an interruption structure (i.e., a large-scale binary form) in the deep middleground.[11] However, along with many other writers, I believe that to privilege the tonal structure over the musical ideas in this manner is one-sided.[12] In fact, Tovey did not go so far in this direction as, owing to his well-known skepticism regarding thematicist logic, is widely believed. To be sure, he pronounced, "There are no rules whatever for the number or distribution of themes in sonata form";[13] however, this assertion is more nearly true than many theorists might wish. For example, although Hepokoski and Darcy poke fun at what they call Tovey's 'throwing-up-one's-hands' approach,[14] their detailed analyses of hundreds of movements actually prove his point. In any case, it's not that Tovey believed that themes don't matter, merely that he denied that any particular types or numbers of themes are 'constituents'—necessary conditions—of sonata form.

A signal advantage of the hermeneutic or genre-based approach to formal analysis is that it offers the possibility of mediating with respect to both of the binary oppositions I mentioned earlier: form as structure vs. as process, and theory vs. practice. Empiricism—practice without theory—is naïve and simplistic at best; many have argued that it is not even possible. Indeed, if Tovey had been a 'pure' empiricist, he would not have been able to write what he did. 'Pure' formalism—theory without practice—may be possible; but even if it were, nobody would be interested in it. Every decent musical work is unique in form; only a patient, empirical analysis can hope to 'get at' what makes it so. At the same time, every musical work instantiates and relates to many types—formal, generic, cultural, and so forth—and, especially in its communicative aspects, can be understood only in awareness of these. This is true notwithstanding the fact that our own historicality—our being embedded in our own time and place and culture, all vastly different from those in which the music under discussion here originated—places an insurmountable barrier between (say) our sense of form and that of Riepel or Koch. It is precisely our historicality that renders unsatisfactory most analyses based primarily on theoretical ideas contemporary with the works being studied. Even if it could be demonstrated that Haydn or Mozart knew and assimilated Riepel's or Koch's theories, the latter cannot serve as templates for understanding their music, for there is no way for us to think ourselves back into the 18th-century milieu in which they learned how to compose—not to mention that their artistic practices encompass universes not dreamed of in any 18th-century theorist's philosophy.

The method that I employ in formal analysis—multivalence—was originally adumbrated (in this guise at least) by the late Harold S. Powers.[15] In multivalent analysis, a musical work is understood as encompassing numerous different 'domains': tonality, musical ideas, rhythm, dynamics, instrumentation, register, rhetoric, 'narrative' design, and so forth.[16] As I wrote telegraphically in the *Revised New Grove Dictionary* (p. 688): "The form is a synthesis of the tonal structure, the sectional and cadential organization, and the ordering and development of the musical ideas." Furthermore, as suggested above, many of these domains must be interpreted not only in terms of 'what happens,' but also dialogically or hermeneutically, in the context of generic expectations and other contextual aspects. This adds what one might whimsically call a meta-multivalent dimension to the analysis.

Multivalence is not theoretically opposed to 'unity,' as some have claimed.[17] But in practice the method entails suspending, at least temporarily, the assumptions that unity is a criterion of value, and that the goal of an analysis is to demonstrate its presence. Insofar as practicable, and despite the inevitable occasional feeling of artificiality, a multivalent analysis should proceed one domain at a time, with little attention to what happens in the other domains, and without preconceptions as to the overall form. (Of course, this ideal can never be entirely realized: we will always 'know' something of what is going on in other domains, always have some advance sense of the overall form; the analyst's mind cannot become a *tabula rasa*.) The temporal patterns that arise in the various domains need not be congruent, and may at times even conflict. When *the* form can be said to exist—often it can't—it necessarily arises from their combination, although how this happens, admittedly, often remains mysterious. On the other hand, the richness and complexity of the greatest music depends precisely on this multifariousness, to which an increased sensitivity can offer ample compensation for the abandonment of reductive unity.

Multivalent analysis as I conceive it is not a theory, but a *method*. Unlike formal theories such as Schenker's '*Ursatz*' or Hepokoski's and Darcy's Sonata Theory, or even Caplin's more nearly informal theory of Classical form, it erects no typologies or grand categorizations, makes no attempt to account for the entirety of any class of works or structures, entails no global claims regarding things that must or must not occur, or which domains are primary (either in general, or in a particular movement or analysis), and so forth. In this sense too it is self-consciously Toveyan.

In what follows, I present two examples of formal analyses in which multivalence plays a prominent role, although in this context I can give only a partial and in some respects tentative view. Both are of very familiar works—Beethoven's Piano Sonata in D major, Op. 10, No. 3, and Mozart's Symphony in C major, K. 551—and in both cases I restrict myself to the exposition of a first movement in sonata form. The formal diagrams in Figures 3.1 and 3.2 present the results of a more or

Measure	1	5	11	17	23	31	38	47	53b	56b	60b	63b	67	71	75	87	94	105b	114	120
Sections	1Gr				Tr + Cad.				2Gr									(Cl.?)	Confirm.	Retr.
Themes	1a	1b	1b	1a	2				3 (motive a'?)				4 (motive a)				5 (≈1)	6	7 (a)	
Caesuras[1]			|	//				|				//					|			|
Harmonies; Structural cadences[2] (upper line)		V	I	$\hat{3}$	vi / ii —— vi – V – I – vii/V – V — I							A:vii—I								
(lower line)			I					V								V	pedal	V	pedal	(V^7)
Antecedent-Consequent	a +	c +	c	a +	c (higher-level)				a +	c +	a +	?	c (higher-level)							
Phrase-rhythm[3]	4 +	6 +	6 +	6	4+4	4+4		16 (=8)	(3 +	4) +	(3 +	2)	4	2+2	3 × 4	8 (=4)	3 × 4	2 × 4	3 × 2 +	4

1. Vertical bold-face line: stable caesuras. Diagonal lines: breaks off in unstable manner.
2. Upper line: lower-level cadences and important harmonic degrees (shown with respect to A as tonic from m. 23 on). Lower line: structural cadences (always reckoning D as tonic).
3. Hypermeter on the two-bar level in bars 38–53a (16 notated downbeats = 8 'real' downbeats) and 87–93 (7 notated downbeats = 4 'real' downbeats).

Figure 3.1 Ludwig van Beethoven, Piano Sonata in D, Op. 10, No. 3, i, exposition: multivalent form

less systematic application of the method: each of the various relevant parameters is presented on a separate and independent time-line, vertically aligned. (Other parameters could be added; for example, dynamics in the sonata, instrumentation in the symphony.)

Beethoven (see Figure 3.1 and Example 3.1).[18] The first caesura comes not in m. 22, when the main theme (shown as bold face **1** in the Figure) breaks off on F♯ (notionally, if not actually, $f\sharp^{3}$, and in this sense the highest note so far) and is followed by a contrasting theme beginning in B minor, but already in m. 16, when it comes to a full cadence followed by a rest. (Measures 1–16 comprise an antecedent plus double consequent: 1a–1b–1b.) Hence mm. 17–22 have a double function: they are *both* an intensified and extended counterstatement of 1a, and therefore the last phrase of the first group—the end of something (as one must conclude from the material and tonality)—*and* a beginning-over, a new antecedent.[19]

This instability at m. 22 forces the music onwards through the entire long succeeding paragraph, all the way to the structural cadence in the dominant in m. 53. In this respect the entire span from m. 1 to m. 53 is a large-scale double period, 1–16 + 17–53. Each period begins with the opening theme, and each consequent is 'more so' than the antecedent: two phrases in the first period, hugely expanded and modulating in the second. However—multivalently—this does not abrogate the first group/transition structure based on contrasting themes and keys, which must be heard as mm. 1–22 + 23–53. Both aspects are present, as complementary aspects of form. In addition, the paragraph concluding in m. 53 is formally unusual. First, the music beginning in m. 23 is harmonically the transition (B minor is the default pivot key between D and A, vi=ii), but its character is that of an important, new, contrasting theme; that is, it functions multivalently as both transition and second theme. And second, this paragraph concludes, not on the 'default' harmonic goal of a half-cadence on V of V (E as dominant of A) but, unusually, with a massive perfect cadence in A. That is, taken as a whole, it is both still transitional, and already second-group-like.[20]

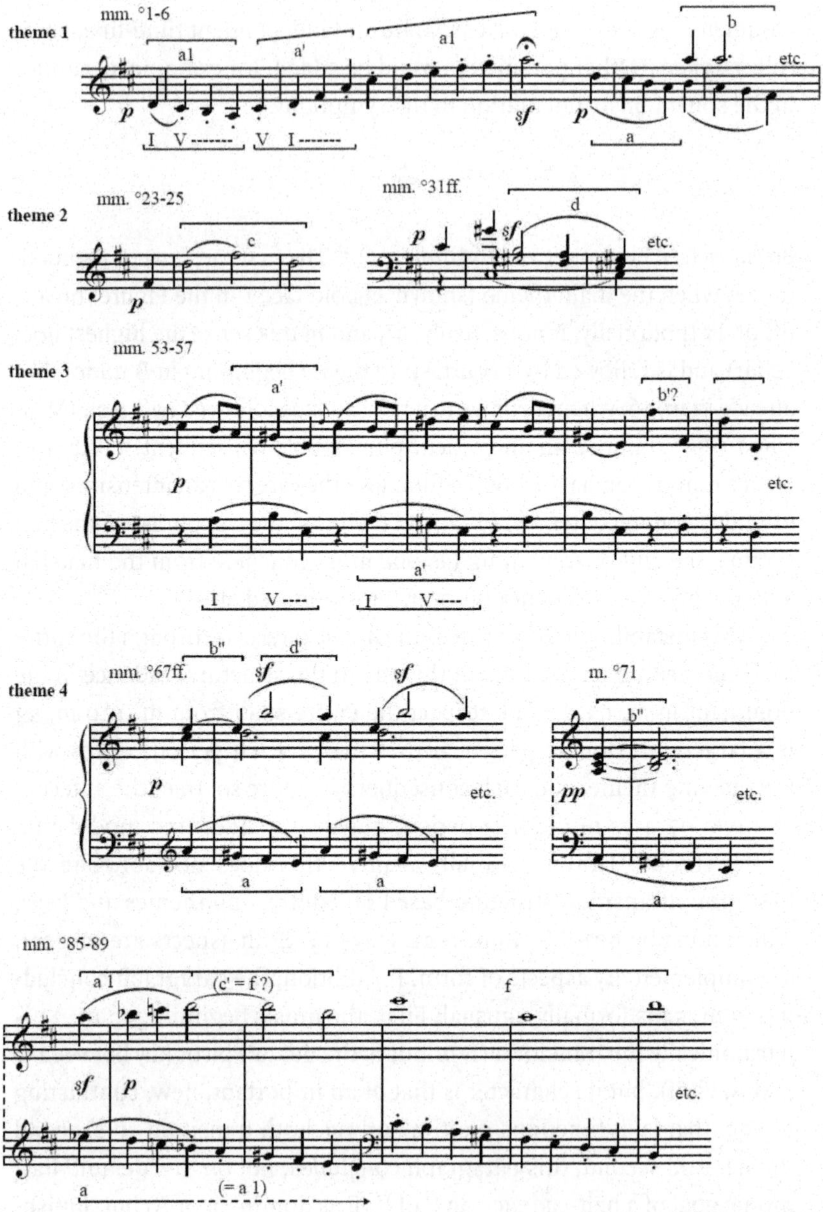

theme 1

mm. °1-6

a1 a' a1 b

p *sf* *p* etc.

I V------- V I-------

a

theme 2

mm. °23-25

c

p

mm. °31ff.

d

p *sf* etc.

theme 3

mm. 53-57

a' b'?

p etc.

a'

I V---- I V----

theme 4

b" d'

mm. °67ff.

sf *sf*

p etc.

a a

m. °71

b"

pp etc.

a

mm. °85-89

a 1 (c' = f ?) f

sf *p* etc.

a (= a 1)

Example 3.1 Ludwig van Beethoven, Piano Sonata in D, Op. 10, No. 3, i, exposition: principal musical ideas

The remainder of the exposition comprises two sections of unequal length. The first, a very long paragraph, comprises themes 3 and 4; it concludes with the PAC in m. 93, but is extended by theme 5 (based on 1) to m. 105. The second, shorter unit comprises the hymn-like theme 6 beginning in m. 105, which cadences after only eight bars, again with extensions (7) until m. 120 or so. Despite the massiveness of the cadence in m. 53, what follows belongs to the second group, not the closing material. In particular, the long theme 4 is not self-sufficient, but dependent on theme 3, which breaks off before reaching its implied cadence. On the other hand theme 4 delays that cadence all the way to m. 93, and thus engenders the biggest climax of the exposition. This relationship between themes 3 and 4 points to a further aspect of overall structure: it is analogous to that between the first group 1 and the transition-plus-cadence 2. In both cases, the initial idea breaks off in an unstable manner, and the subsequent idea uses the resulting potential energy for a massive extension of the expected consequent: mm. 1–53a are answered, not only formally but gesturally, by mm. 53b–93 (or even 53b–105). From this point of view, the massive medial cadence in m. 53 makes sense after all: it establishes the first half of the exposition as both harmonically and gesturally analogous to the second.

Mozart (see Figure 3.2 and Example 3.2).[21] About the first group, I will mention only that it is constructed in a remarkably 'architectonic' manner, in two parallel paragraphs, each of which presents the same ideas (*a*, *b*, *c*) in the same order, and all of whose phrases and periods are clearly marked off by strong cadences and caesuras (mm. 8, 23, 55; the half-cadence at m. 37 is equally strong, but elided with the continuation). The first paragraph moves from I to V, ending with a massive half-cadence in the tonic; the second, somewhat longer, paragraph moves from I through V to V/V, ending with a massive half-cadence in the dominant. (This unusually clear layout is correlated with the fact that in the recapitulation, mm. 1–23 and 36–47 are literally repeated in mm. 189–211 and 225–34, as are 49–55 (transposed) in 237–43.) Unlike the Beethoven, this movement thus exhibits a canonical two-part exposition with medial caesura on V/V, not much less than half way through (55 + 65 measures).

In the second group, by contrast, at *every* cadential arrival the 'flow' continues unbroken to the next idea by elision (except for a local detail in m. 111). On the other hand—this is the kind of thing the multivalent method encourages one to see—the changes in the various domains do not correspond to each other in time. In particular, although the long, quiet, relaxed second theme (*d*) closes with a perfect authentic cadence in m. 71, this event is scarcely marked in the music (except subliminally, as it were, by the entry of motive *b* from the opening theme in the bass). On the contrary, the first break in the flow—and change of topic—is the

First group & transition

	Paragraph 1		Paragraph 2	Par. 1	Par. 2
	1	9 15 19 23	24 36 37 47 49 55	1 19–23	24 49–55
Ideas	a b a b	c/a′ c′	a″/b a″/b/c″ c	a/b c	a/b (a)b — c
Dynamics	***f p f p***	***f***	***p f***	***f/p f***	***p f***
Harm.Prog's	I—V V—I	I——V——	I——ii^6–♯4–V——V/V—— =G: I——ii^6–♯4–V	I——V	I——V/V

Second group

	56/62	71/75	81	87	89	94	98/9	101	111[1]	111/114	117	120
Gesture	Relaxed		Threatening		Vigorous			Buffa		Vigorous/cadential		
Ideas	d	b/d′	e		b″	b″		f		g	c′	
Dynamics	***p***		***f***				***p***			***f***		
Cadences[3]		PAC			PAC	PAC			PAC		PAC (+)	

Harm. Prog's[2] (G): I^6——ii^6 – V – I——IV$^{b\text{-}\natural}$——V— I – ii^6 – V – I——V$^6_5$——I – ii^6 –V – I   I^6 – I— ii^6 – V – I – V – I

1. Although on the phrase-level m. 111 (like the other cadential measures in this second group) is also the beginning of the next phrase by elision, here the downbeat arrival is locally separated off from the offbeat—indeed, second-beat—beginning of the next phrase on I^6.
2. Square brackets designate progressions whose cadences include a strong predominant; braces, those comprising only I–V–I.
3. In this second group it is not easy to determine which of the numerous perfect authentic cadences is the structural cadence (in Cone's sense; cf. the 'EEC' in Hepokoski & Darcy). In part for this reason, I do not hear a separate 'closing group.' Most of those who do so begin it at m. 101 (the *buffa* theme). Schachter, in "Mozart's Last and Beethoven's First" (1991), implies that it coincides with the completion of the deep-middleground 5th-span d^3–g^2 at m. 111.

Figure 3.2 Wolfgang Amadeus Mozart, Symphony in C, K. 551, i, exposition: multivalent form

Example 3.2 Wolfgang Amadeus Mozart, Symphony in C, K. 551, i, exposition: principal musical ideas

eruption of the full orchestra, *forte*, on an ominous C-minor chord in m. 81 (*e*); which is to say, in the middle of a very strong, large-scale I–IV–V–I progression that reaches all the way from m. 75 to m. 89, and concludes with what I hear as the first structural cadence of the exposition. That is, the structural continuity and the gestural discontinuity are out of joint.

In an analogous way, the vigorous continuation beginning in m. 89 with motive *b'* (*b* in diminution) does not cadence (except preliminarily in m. 94); instead, just as it appears to be heading for another structural cadence, it breaks off in m. 98, *piano*, on an unresolved V^6_5 chord—the *piano* astonishingly enters before the caesura—which in turn prepares the next new idea, a *buffa* theme (*f*) that Mozart recycled from his own insertion aria for an opera by Anfossi. Not only is the 'drive towards the cadence' thus denied but, once again, the ostensibly unproblematic harmonic succession (in this case I–V^6_5–I) is correlated with a caesura and with a drastic and unexpected change of topic. Even the next cadence, in m. 111, separates out the downbeat arrival from the unusually long upbeat that begins the following theme (*g*). Hence it is only at the end of the exposition, with the final big cadence in m. 117 and the threefold confirming PACs, that the gestural and harmonic domains are aligned. This movement from 'architectonic' construction in the first group and transition, in which all the parameters are in sync, through a second group that is demonstratively 'out of joint,' to an eventual return to congruence at the end, seems to me the overriding formal principle governing the exposition as a whole.

Before concluding, I shall insert a brief excursus on the term/concept 'closing group.' Notwithstanding its apparent familiarity and the attention paid to it by Caplin and by Hepokoski and Darcy, it remains seriously under-theorized. By definition, if the concluding events in an exposition are heard as a closing theme or group, this must both be separate and distinct from what has preceded it (otherwise we would have no need for the concept), and have actual 'closing' character. However, many writers, particularly those who conceive of the second group as a whole in terms of an overall tonal trajectory towards closure, tend to define the first strong PAC in the dominant as the end of the second group, and therefore construe everything that follows as 'closing.' This is evident in Hepokoski's and Darcy's 'essential expositional closure,' notwithstanding their qualification "first (...) cadence that proceeds onward to differing material" and their sensitive and informed discussion of many alternatives.[22] In many, perhaps most, small- and medium-scale expositions this criterion is unproblematic. But the larger the scale, and the greater the number of distinct ideas (and/or paragraphs) and the greater the degree of differentiation among them, the more likely it is that there will be several strong PACs in the dominant key, *before* the music moves into a specifically closing function; and hence the greater the danger that selection of the first strong PAC (even with the Hepokoski/Darcy qualification) as the division-point between second group and closing group will render the latter unduly long in proportion to the former, and/or label ongoing second-group material inappropriately as 'closing.' For these reasons, I prefer the term and concept 'structural cadence' as the criterion for second-group closure, as adumbrated below. (Admittedly, many later 18th- and early 19th-century theorists treated the second group in just this way. But they tended to think and analyze on a small scale; and from internal evidence it seems clear that they did not have movements such as those I have examined here in mind.)

Thus in the Beethoven sonata, if there were to be a closing theme it could be either theme 5, because this follows the late-second-group PAC and adverts to the opening theme 1—four bars' worth—in something like its original form; or the hymn-like theme 6, with its relaxed and cadential character. Equally plausible to me, however, is a reading in which no separate 'closing group' is invoked at all, but the entire section mm. 53–113 instead heard as a single, large, complex second group: four ideas (3, 4, 5, 6) and three subsections (most likely 53–66, 67–93, 94–113), each different in length, phrasing, and internal construction, which, as a whole, build to a climax towards m. 93, followed by a long, gradual, and multistage process of winding down. Even though m. 93 would seem to be the structural cadence,[23] it is linked to the sequel too strongly to 'count' as the end of the second group; the only unambiguous post-second-group function is the main-theme motive over a tonic pedal in mm. 114ff., which can simply be called a 'codetta.'

Similarly, in the *Jupiter* first movement, given the repeated and complex overlappings between the various domains and the lack of any unambiguous moment of closure until m. 117, I do not find it profitable to distinguish between 'second' and 'closing' groups.[24] As implied above, it is not easy to determine which of the numerous perfect authentic cadences in this second group is the 'structural cadence;' m. 89 is too early, and m. 111 (downbeat) is still *piano*; whereas if the putative closing group begins with the *buffa* theme in m. 101, it is not preceded by a cadence at all! Most analysts who do invoke a closing theme begin it at m. 101 notwithstanding this difficulty, although Carl Schachter multivalently highlights the Schenkerian completion of the deep-middleground 5th-span d^3–g^2 at m. 111 as well.[25] — The entire question deserves a separate study.

These analyses have moved very far from formal models. Despite the apparent 'generic' quality of the stable–unstable–stable construction located in the Mozart, each analysis is individual to its movement and could not be 'generated' by any general notion of exposition construction. The method derives ultimately from the twin traditions of Tovey and Schenker. Indeed Tovey's phenomenological formalism, as I like to call it—as long as it is adequately multivalent, sensitive to context, and so on—is more nearly likely to produce an adequate reading than most others with which I am acquainted.

I have spent the bulk of my analytical time and effort during the last twenty years on Haydn's instrumental and sacred vocal music and Mozart's operas. The lessons have been salutary. Operatic music in particular can be analyzed and understood only in terms of its contexts, specifically the dramatic context. Hence operatic analysis is always to a certain extent ad hoc, driven by the exigencies of the particular case, the particular singer—one could even say: of the moment. In short, operatic analysis is (or should be) distinctly less theory-driven than instrumental analysis has tended to be. Haydn's famous (or notorious) resistance to being subsumed under 'textbook' procedures is equally to the point. I believe that a renewed focus on the particularities and eccentricities of individual works, and their contexts, would be of great benefit to all musical analysis.

Comments on James Webster's Essay "Formenlehre in Theory and Practice"

William E. Caplin

The essay by James Webster raises significant issues for the theory and analysis of musical form. His advocacy of a 'multivalent' analytical approach has proven insightful not only for the two works that he analyzes there, but throughout his numerous writings on classical and romantic music. It is interesting to observe, however, that while his title includes the word 'theory,' its contents largely concern analysis.[1] "Multivalent analysis (...) is not a theory, but a *method*" [>129]. True enough, but this begs the question, what theory of musical form underlies the method? If the theory is not explicitly formulated, it should nonetheless be derivable from analytical practice, and when so derived, must prove to be capable of broader application than the particular case at hand. Thus what is largely missing from Webster's essay is a consideration of the theory that grounds the observations ensuing from his analytical methodology. Indeed, he has generally been reluctant to propose a systematic *Formenlehre*, though he appeals at times to concepts proposed by Tovey and Cone. In what follows, I examine his analytical methodology in light of its theoretical foundations, implicit as they may be. For his analyses raise concerns about his various interpretations of grouping structure and the form-functional consequences arising from those grouping decisions. In particular, his analyses highlight the role of 'thematic content' in determining whether a given group is a formal beginning, middle, or end, and they draw attention to the problem of how broadly the formal categories of 'antecedent' and 'consequent' should be conceived.

Beethoven's Piano Sonata Op. 10, No. 3, i. According to Webster, mm. 17–22 "have a double function: they are *both* an intensified end (...) *and* a beginning-over" [>131]. That this is clearly a form-functional interpretation is evident from his appeal to the temporal qualities of beginning and ending. As Webster makes clear, this group, which I will label as group *y*, is an end in relation to mm. 1–16 (my group *x*) because of continuity in "material and tonality" [>131]. He thus proposes a higher-level group comprising mm. 1–22, as shown by the brackets on the 'Themes' line (third from the top) of his analytical chart (see Figure 3.1). Conflicting with this interpretation (and thus revealing the 'multivalent' aspects of the situation), is the idea that group *y* (mm. 17–22) is an *antecedent* to the following group (my *z*), mm. 23–53, which functions then as a *consequent*. The higher-level group that thus arises (mm. 17–53) is shown in the 'Antecedent-consequent' line (second from the bottom) on his chart.

The idea of a group having a dual formal function, one that usually arises through retrospective reinterpretation, is entirely justifiable given our phenomenological experience of musical time. But when we carefully examine the criteria used to justify this particular form-functional analysis, doubts arise. In the first place, Webster's primary rationale for grouping *x* and *y* together is commonality of thematic content.[2] This seems legitimate enough as a basis for grouping decisions. But the question arises whether we actually experience the last unit (group *y*) of this larger group as expressing a genuine 'end.' At issue is what constitutes the concept of formal ending. I would argue that the experience of formal ending involves the notion of *closure* and, especially, the bringing to conclusion of some *syntactical process*. In the case of a unit that is defined in terms of continuity of thematic content, no such process can be identified: in that group *y* is understood simply to continue the melodic-motivic materials from group *x*, nothing changes, so no sense of closure arises when we arrive at the end of the latter group; there is no necessary reason to believe that the thematic content will change (or not change) after this point. And when it actually happens that the thematic content does change (at the beginning of *z*), we can understand that group *y* was the 'last' of something, but not necessarily reconstruct the experience of its really having 'ended' anything. I would hold that neither continuity of thematic content nor, for that matter, change in thematic content generates the kinds of syntactic processes required to bring about the experience of formal closure. (The same applies to changes in dynamics, texture, and instrumentation; that is, to what Leonard B. Meyer calls the "secondary," or "statistical" parameters of music.)[3] To be sure, this is a complicated issue, one that requires considerably more elaboration than is possible here. But in my estimation, the role of thematic content has been overemphasized as a criterion of formal functionality and raises serious theoretical concerns, as witnessed by my analysis of the *Pastoral* symphony in my opening essay [>35] and by the sonata analysis in Webster's essay.

Let us turn then to Webster's alternative interpretation that group *y* functions as a "beginning over." This view is considerably more sustainable, in that the previous thematic processes are brought to a full conclusion with the home-key perfect authentic cadence at m. 16. So when the music starts up again (incidentally, with the same material that sounded at the beginning of the piece), it is easy to hear a functional beginning at this point. Moreover, as Webster argues, the appearance at m. 22 of a half cadence might raise the possibility of our hearing group *y* as an *antecedent*, whose *consequent*, group *z*, is then stretched out to the perfect authentic cadence at m. 53. The question raised here, however, has to do with the criteria used to define the formal functions of antecedent and consequent. Traditional North-American practice has seen these terms used with such theoretical latitude that almost any 'first' followed by a 'second' is construed to form an antecedent-consequent relationship. Webster's use of these terms seems to follow this practice. In particular, he seems to believe that any unit ending with a half cadence can be understood as an antecedent and that whatever follows this cadence brings a consequent. Problematic in this account, however, is the fact that throughout the classical repertory, a half cadence does not necessarily give rise to either situation. For example, the half cadence found at the end of many development sections does not render the preceding development into a large antecedent, and certainly the recapitulation that follows is not normally construed as a consequent to the development. Similarly, the half cadence found at the end of an expositional transition does not normally promise that the beginning of the subordinate theme that follows will be understood as a consequent to the transition, as antecedent.[4] Indeed, this is precisely the functional situation that I believe obtains in the Beethoven sonata passage. For I would propose that group *y* is the exposition's transition, which, unconventionally, moves to the submediant region for the start of a *modulating* subordinate theme, beginning at m. 23.[5] In this view, the form-functional situation is more complicated than that suggested by Webster. To be sure, we can initially hear group *y* as a new beginning, but when we understand that group *z* itself brings an even stronger sense of 'beginning' (especially in light of the genuine periodic structure of mm. 23–30), we can understand retrospectively that mm. 17–22, as the exposition's transition, expresses a *medial* function, one that stands between the main theme (group x) and the subsequent (first) subordinate theme (z).

Mozart, Symphony No. 41, i. Webster argues that up to m. 55, a variety of musical parameters cluster together to support a grouping structure that sees two broad "paragraphs" (mm. 1–23; 24–55): each ends with a "massive" HC followed by a complete break in rhythmical continuity; each brings the same musical ideas in roughly the same order; and each contains an internal caesura or cadence (mm. 8 and 37) [> Figure 3.2, 135]. He compares this alignment of parameters to what occurs in the second half of the exposition, the "second group" in which a number of the parameters—changes in gesture, ideas, and dynamics—are at odds with the cadential and harmonic processes. Though some of the details of his observations elicit similar theoretical concerns to those that I raised in connection with the Beethoven sonata, I largely agree with his fundamental analytical point. And indeed, the value of such a multivalent analysis truly comes into its own when revealing parametric non-congruencies of this kind. But what must be clearly recognized is that some of these parameters participate in the creation of formal functionality, whereas others do not. In fact, Webster suggests this distinction when he notes that the first "break in the flow" (m. 80) [>134] occurs in the middle of a harmonic progression that concludes with a "structural cadence" (m. 89) [>137]. The effect of this major parametric change is striking precisely because it conflicts with the ongoing form-functional processes defined by harmonic progression and cadence; indeed, Webster in no way proposes that m. 81 marks the beginning of a new "paragraph."

If the situation seems clear enough here, we can reconsider what happens in the first half of the exposition, where the parameters are more in alignment. For in these cases, the impression can be given that texture, rhythmic continuity, thematic content, and dynamics play a defining role in articulating the form-functional situation, namely, the definition of what constitutes a "paragraph." I would argue, on the contrary, that where such parameters may *support* the form-functional articulations, they do not, in themselves, *create* those articulations. Rather, the more 'syntactical' parameters (to speak again with Meyer) of harmonic progression, cadence, and lower-level grouping processes are primarily responsible for engendering the expression of formal functionality. And for this reason, I disagree with Webster's reading of a single "paragraph" embracing mm. 24–55. For the manifest half-cadential articulation at m. 37 and the return of an initiating two-bar basic idea permit us to hear the beginning of a new thematic process (a new "paragraph"), despite the absence of any textural break or any change to 'new' material at this point.[6] I thus hear the music beginning at m. 37 as signaling a clear sense of initiation, not simply a continuation of what was begun back at m. 24.[7] To be sure, the alignment of parameters is clearly stronger here than in the subordinate-theme group (Webster's main point), yet the phrase-structural situation in the first half of the exposition is, in my view, somewhat more complicated than his analysis suggests, due primarily to the more form-defining role of some parameters over others.

Webster's multivalent analyses offer the great advantage of attending to how multiple musical parameters shape a work's form, form being construed here in its broadest sense. But when the analyst confronts the somewhat more limited question of how musical temporality is expressed through various formal functions, then the question of which musical parameters truly participate in this kind of formal shaping comes to the fore. I have argued that only a limited number of such parameters have a direct bearing on the expression of formal function. Thus we must be careful when employing a multivalent approach to make sure that our form-functional readings are firmly grounded in parameters such as harmonic progression, cadence, and grouping processes, while observing how other parameters, such as dynamics, texture, and most especially 'thematic content', either support or rub against such a functional interpretation.

I conclude by noting that my analytical differences with Webster (and, likewise, with Hepokoski) arise not from any fundamental disagreements with his methodology per se, but rather from differences in underlying theory, from the way in which I conceive and define categories of formal organization. If, as I strongly believe, analyses of form are contingent on theories of form, then any eventual reconciliation of divergent formal interpretations awaits consensus on fundamental theoretical perspectives. Though I doubt that such a utopian agreement could ever (or even should) be achieved, a discussion oriented toward underlying theory would help advance our knowledge and understanding of form in this musical repertory. Finally, once we are clear about our theoretical foundations, we can then employ a variety of analytical methodologies—including both multivalent and dialogic approaches—and benefit from how they contribute to a more comprehensive view of musical form.

Comments on James Webster's Essay "Formenlehre in Theory and Practice"

James Hepokoski

James Webster's outline of the issues surrounding the concept of *Formenlehre* and its recent revivals has much to commend it, and he brings both a generous wealth of experience and a great deal of common sense to the table in his discussion. There is much in this essay—particularly his sensitive overview in its initial pages—with which I agree. What will interest the reader here, however, is not a recounting of my many areas of support for Webster's points but rather a look at those portions of the essay for which the Sonata-Theory analytical style would offer differing views. And even here (within a limited space for reply) I shall have no opportunity to elaborate my own conviction that 'Toveyan'-based approaches, which in their ringing declarations were once so influential within English-language analysis, are both inadequate to the tasks at hand and, by now, outdated. Similarly, I shall not enter here into the broader question of how expositional 'closing themes' might properly be identified and grasped, since that matter, replete with often-overlooked nuances and multiple caveats, is dealt with and fully theorized in the *Elements of Sonata Theory*.[1]

Instead, I turn briefly to issues raised in the central portion of Webster's essay, namely the utility of analytical multivalence as demonstrated here—the linear charting of various domains within an individual composition, in part to note their aspects of 'combination' with each other, including their temporal congruence or incongruence as the piece unfolds. One obvious advantage of this approach is that it directs our attention toward textural and thematic features that some earlier styles of analysis had sidelined. This is a concern that Sonata Theory shares. So far as it goes, Webster's multivalent procedure is unexceptionable: it produces a linear set of data, in this case inflected with such Toveyan categories as musical "paragraphs" or first and second "groups." But in practice these charts, accurate as they might be, tell us little that was not obvious in the first place (*forte* here, *piano* there, threatening here, *buffa* there, module *c* here, module *d* there, and so on). In the end, without a conceptual or hermeneutic 'theory' behind them to organize their interpretation into a coherent statement (not at all a 'reductive unity')—or even to encourage them into a deeper, if riskier, reading—this 'method' falls short both in its contentment merely to map out these scattered parameters (a first step advanced, it seems, as a near-final one) and in its subsequent reluctance to harness the data into a more trenchant interpretation of the piece at hand. In the end, one is apparently to be content to say only that within this or that piece the real formal process ('*the* form') in play "often remains mysterious," somehow "necessarily" emerging, though in a way not only beyond our ken but also beyond any strong encouragement toward further speculation, from "[T]he temporal patterns that arise in the various domains" [>129].

Thus Webster's final claim about Op. 10, No. 3, i amounts to little more than what an initial pass-through should tell us at once: "[T]he massive medial cadence in m. 53 makes sense after all: it establishes the first half of the exposition as both harmonically and gesturally analogous to the second" [>134]. In the *Jupiter* symphony, what we ultimately learn is that the "movement from 'architectonic' construction in the first group and transition, in which all the parameters are in sync, through a second group that is demonstratively 'out of joint,' to an eventual return to congruence at the end, seems to me the overriding formal principle governing the exposition as a whole" [>137]. In each case, noting a shape or set of conditions within the "paragraphs" of the acoustic surface seems to be taken as a sufficient explanation of the formal idea that underpins the composition. But these are not yet compellingly formal ideas at all, much less any "overriding formal principle": they are little more than descriptions of what one finds on the surface. They remain underinterpreted data. Bracketed out are the 'why?' and 'so what?' questions. Why and to what larger ends did the composer choose to organize *this* composition in *that* way? What is being suggested, expressed, in this work? How are we to process the larger implications of what we find? And here, of course, we leave the domain of empirically safe, evidentiary 'fact'—one-to-one listings of 'what's there'—and cross the line into the more compelling realm of hermeneutics to take the next interpretive step, to propose responsibly and seriously thought-through, analysis-grounded readings (dialogic readings) that entertain viable approaches (not final answers) to the 'why' and 'so what' questions.

While in the space allotted here I cannot do justice to these matters with regard, for instance, to the *Jupiter* symphony's rich and complex exposition, I might at least suggest the skeletal outlines of a Sonata-Theory view of it—a complementary one, easily merged with Webster's multivalent approach. While this exposition may be dialogically grasped along familiar, two-part/four-zone lines (P TR ' S / C), the treatment of each zone is idiosyncratic, the S / C distinction is indeed problematized (as Webster notes), and many of the curiosities found throughout the exposition result from Mozart's brilliant recastings and exaggerations of normative textural features encountered in the opening bars.

In mm. 1–4, Mozart presents us with a typical *forte-piano*-alternation opening: peremptory *coups d'archet*, tutti (call it $P^{1.1a}$), followed by a completely contrasting, lyrical-warm response in the strings alone ($P^{1.1b}$), a textural pattern neatly paralleled in mm. 5–8, the whole (mm. 1–8) formatted as the presentation of a compound sentence. Nothing unusual so far. What follows, however—as has also been noted by others—is a sonorously grand rhetorical overkill from the tutti—a self-importantly overblown and (surely purposely) empty series of marchlike strides leading to a caesura (though not a *medial* caesura) on an active V, held by a fermata, in m. 23.[2] Mm. 1–23 are then followed by what begins as a *piano*, varied, restatement—like a muffled echo still reverberating in one's memory—that soon drifts off elsewhere (as if 'irresponsibly,' the sentimentalized, sigh-like figures and digressive circle-of-fifths in mm. 31–34) before the stern *tutti* calls things back to order with more inflated rhetorical flourishes starting in m. 37. In Sonata-Theory terms, mm. 1–23 serve as a grand-antecedent P; mm. 24–55 as a TR of the dissolving-consequent type, with a dominant-lock (V/V) secured at m. 49 and a V:HC MC at m. 55.[3]

But merely classifying self-evident action-spaces does not get us very far. Instead, we must look to how those traditional spaces are realized. As Webster has noted, the play of *forte* and *piano*—and of differing rhetorical styles—is crucial. Even more to the point is that the contrasts may be heard as invoking quasi-comically exaggerated, ironized character-types. On the one hand, the *vox auctoritatis*, the urgent bluster of social duty ("Onward! We have a symphony to accomplish!"). On the other hand, the lyrical dreamer wishing to 'stop time,' to seize upon a just-heard figure, to reflect on it, to drift off ('irresponsibly') with it—in short, to fall away from the efficient formal duty of the moment. Proceeding from the initially descriptive to a genuine reading, then, we might propose—as only one possible metaphor—that Mozart staged this exposition as the interplay between these expressively opposed, semi-theatrical types (by no means necessarily implying a masculine-feminine dichotomy), an interplay begun in the pre-MC portion (dominated by the figure of authority) but blossoming to an affectionately drawn series of muddles in the post-MC spaces (dominated by the dreamer-*persona*).

The chromatic head-motive of the lyrical S (mm. 56-57, imitated in the bass, mm. 58-59) may be heard as a wistfully dreamlike memory of the commonly formulaic $\hat{4}$-$\sharp\hat{4}$-$\hat{5}$ (transposed here as $\hat{1}$-$\sharp\hat{1}$-$\hat{2}$) that had pushed vigorously (mm. 48-49) into the just-relinquished dominant-lock (mm. 49-55). The initial S-idea is structured as a politely straightforward parallel period, though with a dallyingly expanded consequent (mm. 56–61, 62–71). It is with the V:PAC at m. 71 that the formal play is nudged into its most subtle and masterly moments. Here, with this first PAC in the new key, we are provided with a generically grounded opportunity for confirming essential expositional closure (EEC), something normally accomplished also with a change of theme and tone. But instead of confirming any such expectation, Mozart's placement of the still-*piano*, $P^{1.1b}$-based motive in the violas and lower strings at mm. 71ff (Webster's motive *b*)—not to mention the continuing second-violin line and the insouciantly carefree upper voice, mm. 72–79—seems to do the opposite. (I note parenthetically that when dealing with such analytical problems, the nuanced approach of Sonata Theory, far from relying woodenly on any automatically mandated 'first-cadence' rule or declaring on behalf of any single solution regarding closure and/or closing themes, urges the analyst instead to explicate the purposeful ambiguities at hand.)[4]

In short, here at m. 71 our *piano* dreamer (or metaphorical equivalent) drifts blithely through this V:PAC, as if heedless to its own cadence, blissfully unaware of its closural implications. This staged inattention—consummate compositional wit, relying on our foreknowledge of standardized generic options—undoes the potential EEC-effect of that

PAC by so unmistakably not fastening it down and proceeding onward to substantially differing material. Moreover, that very inattention is marked by the re-entry of the initial, identifying sign of the dreamer, the $P^{1.1b}$ motive. (Normally, a 'P-based C'—a common onset-of-closing-space marker—would return instead to the *beginning* of P, $P^{1.1a}$, often also with a return to a *forte* dynamic.)[5]

What immediately follows is obvious: a sudden breaking-off ("Oh! Wait! Where am I?" mm. 79–80), a stern *rappel à l'ordre* from the *tutti* (m. 81), recovering the situation by driving 'responsibly' to a more firmly planted, *forte* V:PAC and with it, at m. 89, what may be a staged attempt to produce a 'real' C-like theme with the re-entry of a now-surging, *forte* $P^{1.1b}$. But if this moment seeks to lay claim to launching a P-based C—one interpretive option, with the EEC interpreted as occurring at m. 89—it is entered into with the 'wrong' module, $P^{1.1b}$, the sign of the dreamer, now recovered from its earlier entry and, as if to make amends, inflated into a compensatorily earnest *forte*. It may be that it is because of this modular 'wrongness' that the vigor of this pseudo-C (if that is how we choose to regard it) proves unsustainable.[6] Whatever the reason, it fizzles (cf. m. 79), breaks off on an unlikely V^6_5, and the 'irresponsible' dreamer-aspect takes over once again to fill the gap with a completely *non-sequitur* citation (m. 101) from Mozart's tongue-in-cheek, *buffa* concert aria *Un bacio di mano* K. 541 (with its own implications). Following another V:PAC at m. 111—probably to be construed as the 'real' EEC if one had ultimately discarded the other, wittily problematized option at m. 89—the exposition proper concludes (finally!) with closing-cadential confirmations by the rhetorically full, *forte* orchestra. Deciding where the 'real' EEC is to be placed (mm. 89 or 111?) is not the central analytical point. More important is outlining how and why (to what expressive purpose) Mozart may have dialogically manipulated generic conventions to offer up these multivalently 'out-of-joint' effects that, in turn, lead us into an engaging maze of formal and interpretive ambiguities not to be minimized.

In sum, what Webster's multivalent analysis catalogues in the *Jupiter* exposition is absolutely accurate. I wish only to suggest that the incongruence of textural and formal parameters in the post-MC space of this exposition invites a more provocative, but still analytically responsible, hermeneutic interpretation, one in which the approach of Sonata Theory and its related concerns can help. However modest the claims of this provisional reading might be, it does at least account for every gesture found in this extraordinary exposition, while steering clear of any facile 'unity' assertion.[7]

Response to the Comments

James Webster

Response to William E. Caplin

William E. Caplin states at the beginning of his response that "while [Webster's] title includes the word 'theory,' its contents largely concern analysis" [>140]. This appears to bracket my entire first (and indeed longer) part, devoted to a survey of general notions of form and *Formenlehre*, including related concepts such as structure vs. process; the general vs. the particular; and genres, types, and contexts; if this isn't 'theory,' I don't know what is. By contrast, he is correct when, a few lines later, he notes that I have "generally been reluctant to propose a systematic *Formenlehre*" [>140]. The issue is joined with his assertion regarding my claim that multivalent analysis is a method: "This begs the question, *what theory* of musical form underlies the method? (...) *The theory* (...) *should* (...) be derivable from analytical practice, and when so derived, *must* (...) be capable of broader application (...). What is largely missing (...) is a consideration of *the theory* that grounds the observations (...)" [>140, my italics]. Caplin's comment assumes that analyses and analytical methods *must* be linked to some single, explicitly formulated theory of form (he uses 'theory' always in the singular), and he seems uncertain whether the relation between theory and analysis is top-down and deductive ("underlies the method"; "grounds the observations"), or bottom-up and empirical ("derivable from analytical practice"). By contrast, I don't believe that good analyses and methods need be (explicable as) consequences of or employed as 'data' for *explicit* theories. Even given the obvious truth (which I state in my paper) that there is no such thing a 'purely empirical' analysis—that analysis is 'always already' at least implicitly theoretical—I would reject the notion that, in being so, it must or even should be linked to *some particular, explicitly formulated* theory. Indeed, this is one premise of the multivalent method: in its deliberate attention to multiple domains of the musical work, it invokes, and implicitly utilizes the results of, multiple theories. Nor have I hesitated to name the ones I find most important: Tovey's "phenomenological formalism" (as I call it), Schenker's *Ursatz* theory, a theory of phrase-rhythm (on which Cone has been the most important influence), and others.

I call mm. 1–22 of Beethoven's Op. 10, No. 3 the thematic first group, because they are based on the main theme and are in the tonic (in m. 22, there is at most a potential implication that the high f♯² might be the dominant of B minor), and both mm. 1–4 and mm. 17–22 are antecedents. Caplin objects, on the grounds that we do not "experience" [mm. 17–22] (...) as "expressing a genuine 'end'," because they don't create a sense of closure [>141]. Well, of course they don't!—as my term 'antecedent' after all implies. But the caesura between m. 22 and m. 23 affects not merely the flow, the key, and the register (leap from high to middle), *but the musical material as well*; indeed, what happens in m. 23 entails a radical change of character.[1] Caplin's objection is in my view based on a confusion of domains: his 'beginning/tight—middle/loose—end/cadential' principle here leads him in effect to deny that *any* kind of 'end'-stage in *any* domain could be associated with a formally 'initiating' gesture: "[mm. 17–22 are] the 'last' of something," but [have] "not necessarily (...) 'ended' anything" [>141]. But Beethoven's music cannot be understood in so univalent a manner.

Caplin also problematizes my usage of the terms 'antecedent' and 'consequent.' In this case I must acknowledge that I have not always employed these terms, as well as 'cadence,' as precisely as I should have done.[2] On the other hand I reject the *premises* of his critique of 'antecedent' here, namely (1) that it is applied to overly long spans of music, and (2) that what follows the putative antecedent is not necessarily a consequent. (1) Of course, in traditional analysis 'antecedent' and 'consequent' are applied exclusively or primarily to phrases and periods, on the 4-, 8-, and (at most) 16-bar levels. But in contexts such as Schenker and theories of hypermeter and metrical reduction, no such restriction can be maintained. At most, one could argue for the inclusion of appropriate qualifiers such as 'structural antecedent' (for the first member of a Schenkerian *Ursatz*), 'hypermetrical antecedent,' and so forth. And so, contrary to Caplin's strictures, I may indeed refer to the half-cadence at the end of an expositional transition as bringing a (middleground) antecedent, namely the 'first-group-and-transition,' to a close; and to construe what follows—not necessarily the 'second theme' itself, as Caplin assumes I would have to do, but the entire second group—as a (middleground) consequent. The Mozart exposition offers a crystal-clear example of middleground antecedents and consequents, on an increasingly large scale: mm. {1–22 + 23–55}, and then {1–55 + 56–120}. (All this holds notwithstanding that the resulting middleground periods may be 'antiperiods' (my coinage) or reversed periods, in which the consequent, though indeed closing more strongly than the antecedent, cadences off the tonic.) The same applies to the home dominant at the end of a development section: the first structural 'half' of the movement, 'exposition–and–development,' constitutes the (background) antecedent; the recapitulation, the (background) consequent. (Admittedly, it might be argued that in the latter case the 'true' antecedential cadence is the structural cadence in the dominant at or near the end of the exposition, with the home dominant of the retransition a *re*-capture of this sonority; but this is a distinction that Caplin's account gives no reason to suppose he would care about.)[3]

(2) By contrast, an aspect of my Beethoven analysis that seems to me more nearly open to debate is one that Caplin does *not* address, namely my reading of mm. 23–53 and 67–94 as (expanded) consequents. For mm. 23–53 are not only much longer than 1–22, but based on an entirely different theme and exhibit different modes of compositional procedure and phrase-development, and (as Caplin notes in passing) are modulatory to boot. Thus my interpretation of them as a consequent *tout court* would be a synecdoche of the very kind I elsewhere criticize—taking the middleground harmonic and paragraphing domains as standing for the musical *Formung* in its entirety—were it not that I separate this aspect of my analysis into a domain (analytical line) of its own, which I in no way claim governs the exposition as a whole.

Regarding Caplin's comments on the Mozart: of course, I agree that m. 37 constitutes the most important point of articulation within mm. 24–55, in that it is a clear half-cadence and a clear beginning-over on the initial idea, now oriented around the dominant. Since however mm. 24–37a are too short and uniform (in this context) to qualify as a paragraph, and the continuity of rhythm (elision; not mentioned by Caplin), material, and procedure between mm. 24 and 37 are very strong, I see no advantage in subdividing mm. 24–55 into two separate paragraphs. (Even if one did, the overriding cadential relationship would remain the antecedent-consequent 'rhyme' between the half-cadence and caesura on V in mm. 19–23, and that on V/V in mm. 49–56, both on idea *c*; the overall two-part structure of the 'first–group–and–transition' would remain.) My disagreement of principle is with his *reason* for wishing m. 37 to begin a new paragraph: once again, he asserts a binary opposition between 'primary' or 'form-functional' domains (harmonic progression, cadence, foreground grouping) and 'secondary' or merely 'supporting' ones (texture, rhythmic continuity [vs. discontinuity], thematic content [!], and dynamics). Again: the music of Haydn, Mozart, and Beethoven cannot be understood on the basis of such reductive principles.

Response to James Hepokoski

James Hepokoski's response to my paper confirms my assessment (in my response to his) of the strengths and weaknesses of his approach. In his zeal to promote and defend Sonata Theory as a radically new theory of form, more nearly adequate and qualitatively different than all predecessors, he criticizes earlier and competing theories in an entirely inappropriate manner. It is a matter of opinion whether "Toveyan" approaches are or are not "inadequate" [>146]; however unpersuasive Hepokoski's opinion may be, he is entitled to it as much as I am to mine. But the claim that they are "outdated" [>146] is both false in terms of current practice, and historically simplistic in its assumption that, in an inherently cultural and subjective practice such as music (and its analysis), so important and long-standing a tradition ever becomes *inherently* outdated, or (a related point) will never experience a revival.[4] In any case, as I state repeatedly and is obvious from my own practice, the Toveyan approach is only one of numerous different systems and theories I employ.

By contrast, his critique of multivalent analysis (as represented by my examples here) demands attention. Essentially, it makes two assertions. (1) The results are empirical and elementary: "tell us little that was not obvious in the first place"; "falls short both in its contentment merely to map out (...) parameters (...) and in its (...) reluctance to harness the data into a more trenchant interpretation"; and so forth [>146-147]. (2) They are insufficiently hermeneutic: "[T]hey are little more than (...) underinterpreted data. Bracketed out are the 'why?' and 'what?' questions. Why (...) did the composer (...) organize *this* composition *this* way? What is being suggested, expressed (...)? Here, we leave the domain of empirically safe, evidentiary 'fact' (...) and cross the line into the more compelling realm of hermeneutics"; and so forth [>147]. Although these aspects are conceptually and methodologically distinct, Hepokoski treats them as interrelated, indeed as two aspects of a single issue. (It should be noted that whereas the term 'surface' ordinarily refers to the musical foreground—as opposed to a Schenkerian background, a Schoenbergian *Grundgestalt*, or 'subthematic' motivic relations—in Hepokoski's comment it connotes observational and empirical analysis, as opposed to hermeneutic interpretation.)

(1) Of course, the analytical results in my paper are based on observation, and are represented diagrammatically in terms of the musical foreground. But they are neither merely empirical nor obvious. Not merely empirical, because (as has been asserted repeatedly by all three authors) no analytical practice can be so; as stated above, my own is based on a number of well-established theories about form and process in tonal music. It is not clear to me how Hepokoski can suppose that analyses that discuss alternatives regarding, but do not answer, questions such as the location of the structural cadence or the presence of a distinct closing group are "merely empirical." And certainly not "obvious":[5] my reading of the Beethoven exposition as an enormous double period, each with a vastly expanded and non-parallel consequent, with

multivalent functionings of mm. 17–22 and 23–53, was new when first published, and in no sense constitutes mere "underinterpreted data." Hepokoski's dismissal of my "final claim" as "little more than what an initial pass-through should tell us at once" ignores this larger argument [>147]. (Indeed, as I noted in my response to his paper, Hepokoski's own analytical observations are remarkably matter-of-fact, far below any standard implied by his critique of mine.)

(2) Thus Hepokoski's real complaint is the lack of hermeneutic interpretation in my analyses. Indeed, there is little of this: I did not take it as my brief to pursue such questions here, but focused rather on aspects of form and *Formenlehre* in their own right. But (as he well knows) I am the last person to reject interpretation on principle, or to eschew it in my own work. Be this as it may: Hepokoski is of course free to explore the "more compelling realm" of hermeneutics in his own practice [>147], and to value writings in which they appear more highly than those in which they do not. It is however a capital error to suppose that, to be adequate to its purpose, an analysis (even a formal analysis of an entire movement) *must* explicitly raise interpretative issues—as wrongheaded as it would be to suppose that an 18th-century symphony, to count among the best of its kind, *must* pursue overt cyclic integration, or *explicitly* entail 'extramusical' aspects. (This is not to deny that every analysis 'tells a story,' or that many (all?) analyses *implicitly* suggest interpretative aspects, any more than to deny that non-programmatic 18th-century symphonies were *implicitly* related to the world outside them, by their use of 'topics,' conventions, and so forth.)[6]

To turn to the Mozart (the main example in Hepokoski's critique): I do not believe that his comments either make a convincing case for the inadequacy of my analysis, or add very much to the larger understanding of this movement. His dismissal of my conclusion regarding the form of the exposition (telegraphically: architectonic—unstable and multivalent—congruent) as "not (...) compellingly formal ideas at all, much less any 'overriding formal principle': they are little more than descriptions" seems to depend on an arcane, and certainly unstated, notion of what might constitute a 'formal idea.'[7] On the contrary (as Caplin for his part well knows), the paradigm: 'stable beginning—unstable middle—stable end' is as old, and basic, a formal principle as any we know, which does not lose its pertinence merely because it is particularized in a given discussion of a single movement. To be sure, Hepokoski's 'complementary' discussion of this exposition, especially the first group and transition, is more detailed than mine. However, mine was (again) intended as a 'demonstration example' of the multivalent method and the kinds of analytical (not interpretative) results it fosters, not as a full-dress account of the movement as a subject in its own right.

As for the substance of Hepokoski's analysis/interpretation, it goes without saying that it is correct,[8] with many interesting details; the interpretative aspects (the authority figure vs. the 'dreamer,' and so forth)[9] are engaging and (as always in the best cases) themselves suggestive of further analytic moves. However, it is not clear to me that much is actually gained *analytically*: in this case, surely, if one were to infer a form-diagram of the movement from the prose description, it would look scarcely different from mine. And so (as always) it is for the reader to decide, whether and to what extent the analytical-interpretative results justify the rhetoric employed on their behalf.

Notes

FORMENLEHRE IN THEORY AND PRACTICE

James Webster

1. Kurt Westphal, *Der Begriff der musikalischen Form in der Wiener Klassik: Versuch einer Grundlegung der Theorie der musikalischen Formung* (1935).

2. Edward T. Cone, *Musical Form and Musical Performance* (1968), pp. 88–98 (the quoted passage is on p. 89).

3. James Webster, "Sonata Form," in *The Revised New Grove Dictionary* (London, 2001), Vol. 23, p. 688, col. 1. (I quote my own article not out of hubris or excessive self-regard, but simply because in it my ideas are formulated more efficiently than elsewhere.)

4. Mark Evan Bonds, *Wordless Rhetoric: Music and the Metaphor of the Oration* (1991), pp. 13–30.

5. As I argue in *The Revised New Grove Dictionary*, pp. 689–90 (as does Caplin in his essay here). Many of those who disagree with my approach give the impression of doing so owing to a belief that I employ sonata form as a criterion of *value*. Admittedly, in the past there was a strong tendency in this direction; but I don't share it, and I see no reason to alter the approach that seems to me best merely for that reason.

6. As argued in Hepokoski & Darcy, *Elements of Sonata Theory*, pp. 343–45.

7. Most commonly cited is *Realism in Nineteenth-Century Music* (1985), p. 121 et passim; with respect to sonata form, see *Analysis and Value Judgment* (1983), pp. 45–46 et passim. For a critique of Dahlhaus's usage (not of the concept as such) see Philip Gossett, "Carl Dahlhaus and the 'Ideal Type'" (1989-90), pp. 49–56.

8. For simplicity's sake, I do use the single word 'form' thereafter.

9. Jeffrey Kallberg, "The Rhetoric of Genre: Chopin's Nocturne in G Minor" (1988), pp. 238–61; James Hepokoski, "Genre and Content in Mid-Century Verdi" (1989), pp. 249–76.

10. Dahlhaus once published what he imagined to be a provocative study under the title "'Dritte Themen' in Clementis Sonaten? Zur Theorie der Sonatenform im 18. Jahrhundert" (1982), pp. 444–61, as if there were anything unusual or problematic in having more than two important themes or sections in an exposition. On close inspection his writings on form in his Beethoven monograph, for example, prove to be grounded on 'thematicist' principles; see James Webster, "Dahlhaus's *Beethoven* and the Ends of Analysis" (1993), pp. 205–27. The term 'thematicism' is taken from Joseph Kerman, *Contemplating Music* (1985), pp. 64–79.

11. Heinrich Schenker, *Free Composition* (1979), §§ 87–99 and Exx. 21–26; § 192; §§ 309–16 (with the long gloss by Oster, pp. 139–41) and Exx. 153–54.

12. Regarding Schenker, see, for example: James Webster, *Haydn's Farewell Symphony and the Idea of Classical Style* (1991), pp. 50–56.

13. Donald F. Tovey, *Musical Articles from the Encyclopaedia Britannica*, p. 210.

14. Hepokoski & Darcy, *Elements of Sonata Theory*, p. 8.

15. Harold S. Powers, unpublished study of Verdi's *Otello* presented at a Verdi–Wagner conference at Cornell University in 1984 (for the published papers

see Carolyn Abbate and Roger Parker (eds.), *Analyzing Opera: Verdi and Wagner* (Berkeley, 1989). For detailed expositions of the method, see Webster, "The Analysis of Mozart's Arias" (1991), pp. 101–99; id., "The Form of the Finale of Beethoven's Ninth Symphony" (1992).

16. Note the inclusion of so-called 'secondary' parameters (dynamics, instrumentation, register), which are usually marginalized in the analysis of 18th-century instrumental music (Mahler, say, being a different story). For an example in which register is treated as equivalent in importance to tonal structure, see my analysis of the first movement of Haydn's string quartet Op. 9, No. 4, in "Haydn's Op. 9: A Critique of the Ideology of the 'Classical' String Quartet" (2005), pp. 149–50. (I note in passing that in a vocal work one must go further, adding (at least) the verbal text, differences of material, rhythm, etc. between voice(s) and accompaniment, vocal *tessitura*, and temporal and functional relations between vocal passages and those for instruments alone. Furthermore, a text is multivalent in its own right: it comprises (at least) the poetic form, linguistic and lexical usages, tone and voice, and ideational content—not to mention the complex and difficult issues of the relation of text to music, and of interpretation, that inevitably arise.)

17. E.g., William Kinderman, *Beethoven* (1995), pp. 313–15.

18. This analysis is condensed and adapted from Webster, "Dahlhaus's *Beethoven*" (1993), pp. 216–26.

19. This is clear among other ways from the tonality: the high $f\sharp^2$ in m. 22 is reinterpreted as the dominant of B minor, in which the next paragraph begins.

20. See the comments on this second group in Hepokoski & Darcy, *Elements of Sonata Theory*, p. 176.

21. A version of this analysis was presented at a plenary session on Mozart, held at the annual meeting of the Society for Music Theory, Los Angeles, November 2006.

22. *Elements of Sonata Theory*, p. 120.

23. On this concept see Edward T. Cone, "Analysis Today" (1960), pp. 174–75, 181–83.

24. Hepokoski and Darcy acknowledge that this second group presents difficulties in this regard, without mentioning particulars (*Elements of Sonata Theory*, p. 159).

25. Carl Schachter, "Mozart's Last and Beethoven's First," (1991), pp. 239, 241.

COMMENTS ON JAMES WEBSTER'S ESSAY "FORMENLEHRE IN THEORY AND PRACTICE"

William E. Caplin

1. The same can be observed for James Hepokoski's essay "Sonata Theory and Dialogic Form."

2. He also speaks of tonality playing a role, but this is questionable since group *y* can most reasonably be seen to end with a half cadence on the dominant of VI, thus suggesting a modulation away from the home key.

3. Leonard B. Meyer, *Style and Music: Theory, History, and Ideology* (1989), pp. 14–16, 208–211.

4. Indeed, if we believed so, then we would regularly have to group the transition with the subordinate theme, which would fly in the face of the traditional notion of a 'two-part exposition,' which sees the former function as the end of the first part, and the latter function, the beginning of the second part.

5. On the notion of modulating subordinate theme, see *Classical Form*, p. 119.

6. Interpreting the broader form-functional situation in mm. 24–55 is somewhat complicated, but one reading would see that mm. 24–37 significantly destabilize the harmonic and phrase-structural environment, and so this group can be viewed as a transition in relation to mm. 1–23 as main theme. What follows at m. 37 can then be understood as the second part of a 'two-part transition' (see *Classical Form*, p. 135).

7. The *forte* dynamic at m. 37 supports this sense of beginning but is not, in itself, responsible for it.

COMMENTS ON JAMES WEBSTER'S ESSAY "FORMENLEHRE IN THEORY AND PRACTICE"

James Hepokoski

1. *Elements of Sonata Theory*, pp. 120–31, 150–70, 180–94.

2. Relevant here is Carl Dahlhaus's remark in "Issues in Composition," *Between Romanticism and Modernism* (1980), pp. 43–44: "In the first movement of Mozart's C major Symphony, K. 551, the continuation of the first thematic period—a tutti described by Hans Georg Nägeli [Stuttgart, 1826] as 'shallow' and 'trivial'—can be justified by its function, which is to provide a counterbalance to the opening of the movement, even if it is indefensible in terms of melodic or harmonic invention, of which it has none. Classical form could survive banality in some (not all) of its parts." Cf. also Leonard G. Ratner, *Classic Music: Expression, Form, and Style* (1980), p. 103, who noted the initial contrasts of *coups d'archet* and 'singing style'—which, taken together, "create a sense of compression that explodes into a broad ['march'] extension"; and Elaine Sisman, *Mozart: The Jupiter Symphony* (1993), pp. 40, 47–48, describing the 'grand style' of the opening eight bars, followed by the return of "the big tutti (...) now with a definite fanfare-like march rhythm."

3. On the concept of the grand antecedent, of which this passage is a touchstone, see: Hepokoski & Darcy, *Elements of Sonata Theory*, pp.77–80; for TR of the dissolving-consequent type, see pp. 101–02. The term V:HC MC does not mean that there is a half-cadence at m. 55; rather, the HC (or dominant arrival) occurs at m. 49, and the subsequent MC is 'built around' the V:HC via a typical dominant-lock extension (*Elements of Sonata Theory*, pp. 24–27).

4. See note 1 above as well as the dozens of pages in the *Elements of Sonata Theory* flagged in its index under the entry "flexibility in analysis, terminology, and interpretation" (p. 657). It is one of Sonata Theory's advantages that, instead of offering simple, declarative solutions to difficult cases, it is com-

mitted instead to seeking to "explicate the [formal] ambiguity"—that is, to describe with some precision exactly why one experiences an ambiguity at this or that moment of the structure. (In most cases, we also think that such ambiguities are probably intentional, a richly intricate aspect central to the composition under analysis.)

5. *Elements of Sonata Theory*, pp. 184–85, outlines the style and typical role of the P-based C, one of the most important (though not invariable) formal markers of the idiom. Cf. also p. 140–41 on occurrences of P- or TR-material in the interior of S-zones.

6. Alternatively, perhaps its basis-in-P has by now been wittily overused, its potential for an unflagging C-power already spent? Or perhaps we are to conclude that for all of our cadences and strenuous, *forte* efforts we have not yet managed to leave S-space behind, since the $P^{1.1b}$ module had already been marked with S-qualities in m. 71?

7. Cf. *Elements of Sonata Theory*, pp. 251–54, the subsection entitled, "Narrative Implications: The Sonata as Metaphor for Human Action."

RESPONSE TO THE COMMENTS

James Webster

1. A point correctly emphasized by Dahlhaus (whose often one-sided focus on themes and their characters in this case alerted him to something important), who reads the exposition as presenting four contrasting thematic characters in succession: '*marcato*,' '*cantabile*' (m. 23), '*scherzando*' (m. 53), and '*hymnic*' (m. 106); see Dahlhaus, *Ludwig van Beethoven: Approaches to his Music* (1991), pp. 129–31.

2. See the well-founded critique of my calling m. 8 of Haydn's *Oxford* Symphony a 'half-cadence,' in Caplin's "The Classical Cadence: Conceptions and Misconceptions" (2004), pp. 83–86 (although I would reject his other criticisms of my usage of 'cadence' in this passage and elsewhere in the same article).

3. There is a large, if not yet thoroughly digested, literature on this issue in the Schenkerian tradition, which there would be no point in citing here.

4. When I was a graduate student, a then already well-known and now distinguished emeritus professor opined to me that Tovey's writings were "little more than bedtime reading." Today, along with many others who then thought themselves more 'advanced' than Tovey, he knows better. On the issue of how and why critical writings (such as Tovey's, Kerman's, and Rosen's) may become 'dated' (a preferable concept to "outdated"), see Webster, "Rosen's Modernist Haydn" (2008), pp. 287–88.

5. To judge by comparisons of my results with other published ones, see the references in my paper (to which, on the Mozart, one might add those given in Hepokoski's response to me, note 2 [>161]).

6. For my views on these matters, see Webster, *Haydn's* Farewell *Symphony* (1991), pp. 5–7, 112–19, 247–51, 284–87 et passim (with applications throughout the volume).

7. There is no entry for this or any comparable term in the index to *Elements of Sonata Theory*.

8. Misleading, however, is the characterization of mm. 1–8 as "the presentation of a compound sentence"; what is meant is the 'presentation' *component* of a compound sentence (which as a whole comprises mm. {1–8 + 9–23}. The first eight bars as such are of course an antecedent–consequent period, in which each half has contrasting subphrases and the 'opposite' harmonic orientation.

9. Even the supposedly 'outdated' Tovey described this opposition in comparable terms. Indeed, whereas Hepokoski's "*vox auctoritatis*, the urgent bluster of social duty (...) lyrical dreamer" [>148-149] is drawn more or less out of thin air (and 19th-century air at that), Tovey more pertinently invokes the world of 18th-century opera: "A Mozart architectural opening [is] not merely architectural. On the contrary, most of its formulas were originally dramatic. The formula [here] is [...] the tyrant on his throne brandishing his sceptre while the humble suppliant pleads at his feet" (Donald F. Tovey, *Beethoven* (1944), pp. 86–87; compare id., *Essays in Musical Analysis*, Vol. 1 (1935), p. 196).

Epilogue
The Future of Formenlehre

Pieter Bergé

The main objective of the present volume was to confront different theories and methodologies of musical form. The three authors invited to participate in this discussion—William E. Caplin, James Hepokoski and James Webster—were requested first to present their own fundamental positions on the subject, then to critique the viewpoints of their colleagues, and finally to refute—or, eventually, incorporate—the comments on their own opening essays that their peers had put forward.[1] This rather unusual procedure of 'direct' engagement has clearly stimulated the participants to support their theoretical and methodological premises with the greatest possible rigor. Especially in the *Response* essays, the tendency to provide a thoroughgoing clarification of their differing theoretical foundations is strikingly manifest, and for good reasons. For in the *Comments*, the opposing authors did not refrain from highlighting what they considered to be inconsistencies or anomalies in the theories and methods of their colleagues. Furthermore, the authors often could not resist the temptation of presenting their own analytical interpretations of compositions that had been discussed in the opening essays. By doing so, they could not only reveal the presumed deficiencies in the practical applications of their colleagues' theories and methods, but also show how their own approaches could possibly rectify, or compensate for, these shortcomings.

The aim of this *Epilogue* is not to recapitulate the discussions presented in the preceding essays. After all, such a summary would only diminish the original vivacity of the debates and pitifully neutralize the (quite revealing) stylistic idiosyncrasies of the protagonists. Rather, the intention here is to reflect on how the three positions defended in this book can be approached from an *external* point of view. Such a perspective starts from the observation that, quite often, comparisons among different analytical approaches get stuck prematurely in a needlessly unilateral urge to defend one specific theory or method. Typically enough, this attitude is frequently characterized by a tendency to repudiate competing theories by over-emphasizing what these theories do *not* elaborate (or what they do not *sufficiently* elaborate). Theories and methods, however, should not be evaluated on the basis of what they deliberately omit from their analytical perspectives. On the contrary, any valuable critique has to render a full account of what a theory or method *positively* aspires to. Furthermore, one should be extremely cautious not to confuse the fundamentals of a given theory with its concrete working out. The refutation of some specific elements within a theoretical framework should not necessarily imply the rejection of that theory itself; and, conversely, the fundamental disapproval of a general theory must not include the general denial of its constituting elements. Obvious as this may seem, the confusion described here arises all too frequently, in most cases dictated by a fruitless insistence on asserting the supremacy of one specific approach over another. The question of what extra value such an imagined hegemony could possibly yield is thereby, astonishingly, disregarded.

Moreover, the attitude of claiming theoretical supremacy is not just unfounded, it is paradoxical too. For it fails to consider that the intrinsic value of any theory surely depends on the relevance of its *restrictions*. Theories have the capacity of breaking new ground and delivering innovative insights *only* if they succeed in creating a framework that enables the exhaustive elaboration of their chosen premises. The one-sidedness of a theory, therefore, is not a defect, but a necessity, a *conditio sine qua non*. By recognizing this limitation, we acknowledge the appropriateness of embracing differing theories in the effort to grasp the complexity of a given phenomenon, *however incompatible these theories may be.*

By accepting the invitation to participate in the Freiburg EuroMAC *Formenlehre* session in October 2007, and by even taking up the challenge to elaborate on that session in the discussions presented in this volume, Caplin, Hepokoski and Webster indirectly have expressed their approval of this basic attitude. More importantly, the theoretical positions they espouse in this book—different as they may be—subscribe to this mindset in a more direct manner as well. Caplin, for instance, insists that his theory of classical form is essentially a theory of formal *functions*, and that "only a limited number of (...) parameters have a direct bearing on the expression of formal function" [>144]. This restriction, however, is a purely 'intra-theoretical' factor: it holds no implications for which parameters in *music* would be more important than others. But even with respect to music *theory*, Caplin openly advocates the benefits of "employ(ing) a variety of analytical methodologies," as long as these methodologies have clear and well-circumscribed theoretical foundations [>145]. He thus acknowledges the relevance of other theoretical approaches, precisely because the scope of his own theory is so consciously and rigorously delimited.

Hepokoski's receptivity toward other theoretical approaches is somewhat less explicit. His (and Darcy's) 'open' attitude is more or less *implied* in the concept of dialogic form itself. Whereas Sonata Theory—as a theory—clearly aspires to take into account all 'elements' that, in some way or another, constitute form in late eighteenth-century sonatas, the underlying method of dialogic form implies the necessity of broadening the conceptual context in which that theory resides. As a dialogical process, Sonata Theory refuses to be intrinsically self-contained: it welcomes all types of external theoretical considerations (historical, hermeneutic, and so forth), assuming that these can refine the interpretation of formal organization. Sonata Theory is, so to speak, fundamentally integrative.

Finally, Webster's idea of multivalent analysis is based, in its very essence, on the conviction that music is too complex a phenomenon to be explained or interpreted in a satisfactory manner by holding to a single analytical approach. Webster thus renounces the objective of developing either a 'restrictive' (cf. Caplin) or an 'integrative' (cf. Hepokoski) theoretical model. His approach rather starts from the idea that *all* musical parameters should be investigated in their own right so as to grasp the general '*Form*' and '*Formung*' of a composition. Such an attitude evidently includes a basic readiness to confront all possible theoretical strategies that can illuminate one or more aspects of musical form. From that point of view, multivalent analysis can be understood as a fundamentally 'non-exclusive' approach.

As stated above, the incompatibility of different theoretical and analytical models represents an opportunity rather than an inconvenience. The interpretation of musical form *needs* differing and irreconcilable theoretical approaches, just as music theory in general needs to 'celebrate' the contradictions, dissimilarities, and paradoxes that characterize the internal diversity of musical phenomena. But a celebration is fundamentally different from a mere 'acceptance.' To celebrate means to activate differing views on identical data in order to deconstruct the inner complexity and richness of all sorts of musical phenomena. It further implies an attitude that refrains from conceited claims of theoretical supremacy. Ideally, such a celebration would even embrace those traditions of research that are often blamed for having caused the relative constraining of the study of musical form in the second half of the twentieth century.[2]

Of course, no progress in the study of musical form can be made by a mere accumulation of irreconcilable interpretations. The gathering of competing views only makes sense if there exists a fundamental willingness to investigate the individual theoretical status of any given theory or method. Such an attitude compels all music theorists and analysts to question constantly the restrictions of their own approach, to consider what specific lacunae these restrictions entail within their own theories, and to ascertain if—and to what extent—these inherent shortcomings can be compensated by theories based on different premises. To accept that threefold responsibility, and especially, to implement it in all possible contexts of musical education is surely one of the greatest challenges for the future of *Formenlehre*.

Notes

1. The events described here refer to the genesis of the present volume, not to the order in which the essays are presented.

2. For example, see Caplin, *Classical Form*, p. 3: "Once a venerable subdiscipline of music theory, the traditional *Formenlehre* (...) has largely been abandoned by theorists and historians for many reasons. These include the influence of Heinrich Schenker's critique of form as foreground manifestation of more fundamental contrapuntal-harmonic processes; the acceptance of a historicist attitude that eighteenth-century music is best analyzed by eighteenth-century theories; and the mistrust by the new musicology of systematic, classificatory models of musical organization." Two of these reasons are also endorsed by James Webster in the beginning of his essay in the present volume: "During the second half of the twentieth century, theories of musical form were by and large considered passé in English-speaking countries, whether by Schenkerians (especially orthodox Schenkerians) who believed that they had overcome bad old analytical traditions; or by postmodern writers, who tend to disdain analysis of 'the music itself' altogether" [>123]. Another inhibiting factor in the development of theories of musical form—the so-called 'war against the textbooks'—is raised by Hepokoski and Darcy in *Elements of Sonata Theory* (pp. 6–9). These authors rightly observe that in the second half of the twentieth century, "[T]he reiterated conviction that there was no single plan for sonata form in the later eighteenth century" caused an attitude in which the inquiry into "the presence of substantially more complex systems of standard practices" was discouraged (p. 7).

Bibliography

Abbate, Carolyn & Roger Parker (eds.), *Analyzing Opera: Verdi and Wagner*. Berkeley: University of California Press, 1989.

Agawu, V. Kofi, *Playing with Signs: A Semiotic Interpretation of Classic Music*. Princeton: Princeton University Press, 1991.

Bergé, Pieter (ed.), William E. Caplin & Jeroen D'hoe (co-eds.), *Beethoven's* Tempest *Sonata. Perspectives of Analysis and Performance* (Analysis in Context. Leuven Studies in Musicology, Vol. 2). Leuven: Peeters, 2009.

Bonds, Mark Evan, *Wordless Rhetoric: Musical Form and the Metaphor of the Oration*. Cambridge: Harvard University Press, 1991.

Caplin, William E., "Structural Expansion in Beethoven's Symphonic Forms," in William Kinderman (ed.), *Beethoven's Compositional Process*. Lincoln: University of Nebraska Press, 1991, pp. 27–54.

Caplin, William E., *Classical Form: A Theory of Formal Functions for the Instrumental Music of Haydn, Mozart, and Beethoven*. New York: Oxford University Press, 1998.

Caplin, William E., "The Classical Cadence: Conceptions and Misconceptions," *Journal of the American Musicological Society*, 57/1(2004), pp. 51–118.

Cone, Edward T., "Analysis Today," *Musical Quarterly*, 36(1960), pp. 172–88.

Cone, Edward T., *Musical Form and Musical Performance*. New York: Norton, 1968.

Cook, Nicholas, "The Other Beethoven: Heroism, the Canon, and the Works of 1813–14," *19th-Century Music*, 27(2003), pp. 3–24.

Dahlhaus, Carl, *Between Romanticism and Modernism* (trans. Mary Whittall). Berkeley: University of California Press, 1980 [orig. published in German, 1974].

Dahlhaus, Carl, "'Dritte Themen' in Clementis Sonaten? Zur Theorie der Sonatenform im 18. Jahrhundert," *Annales musicologiques*, 21(1982), pp. 444–61.

Dahlhaus, Carl, *Analysis and Value Judgment* (trans. Siegmund Levarie). New York: Pendragon Press, 1983 [orig. published in German, 1970].

Dahlhaus, Carl, *Realism in Nineteenth-Century Music* (trans. Mary Whittall). Cambridge: Cambridge University Press, 1985 [orig. published in German, 1982].

Dahlhaus, Carl, *Ludwig van Beethoven: Approaches to his Music* (trans. Mary Whittall). Oxford: Oxford University Press, 1991 [orig. published in German, 1987].

Deane, Basil, "The French Operatic Overture from Grétry to Berlioz," *Proceedings of the Royal Musical Association* 99 (1972-1973), pp. 67–80.

Drabkin, William, *Beethoven: Missa Solemnis*. Cambridge: Cambridge University Press, 1991.

Fillion, Michelle, "Sonata Exposition Procedures in Haydn's Keyboard Sonatas," in Jens Peter Larsen, Howard Serwer & James Webster (eds.), *Haydn Studies. Proceedings of the International Haydn Congress, Washington, D.C., 1975*. New York: Norton, 1981, pp. 475–81.

Galand, Joel, "*Formenlehre* Revived," *Intégral*, 13(2001), pp. 143–200.

Gossett, Philip, "Carl Dahlhaus and the 'Ideal Type,'" *19th-Century Music*, 13(1989–90), pp. 49–56.

Hatten, Robert S., *Musical Meaning in Beethoven: Markedness, Correlation, and Interpretation*. Bloomington: Indiana University Press, 1994.

Hepokoski, James, "Genre and Content in Mid-Century Verdi," *Cambridge Opera Journal*, 1(1989), pp. 249–76.

Hepokoski, James, "Back and Forth from Egmont: Beethoven, Mozart, and the Nonresolving Recapitulation," *19th-Century Music*, 25(2001), pp. 127–54.

Hepokoski, James, "Beyond the Sonata Principle," *Journal of the American Musicological Society*, 55(2002), pp. 91–154.

Hepokoski, James & Warren Darcy, *Elements of Sonata Theory: Norms, Types, and Deformations in the Late-Eighteenth-Century Sonata*. New York: Oxford University Press, 2006.

Iser, Wolfgang, *The Act of Reading: A Theory of Aesthetic Response*. Baltimore: Johns Hopkins University Press, 1978 [orig. published in German, 1976].

Johnson, Douglas et al., *The Beethoven Sketchbooks*. Berkeley: University of California Press, 1985.

Kallberg, Jeffrey, "The Rhetoric of Genre: Chopin's Nocturne in G Minor," *19th-Century Music*, 11(1988), pp. 238–61.

Kerman, Joseph, *Contemplating Music*. Cambridge: Harvard University Press, 1985.

Kinderman, William, "Beethoven's Symbol for the Deity in the *Missa Solemnis* and the Ninth Symphony," *19th-Century Music*, 9(1985), pp. 102–18.

Kinderman, William, *Beethoven*. New York: Oxford University Press, 1995.

Larsen, Jens Peter, "Sonata Form Problems," in Jens Peter Larsen, *Handel, Haydn, and the Viennese Classical Style* (trans. Ulrich Krämer). Ann Arbor: UMI Research Press, 1988 [orig. published in German, 1963], pp. 269–79.

Lerdahl, Fred & Ray Jackendoff, *A Generative Theory of Tonal Music*. Cambridge: MIT Press, 1983.

Lerdahl, Fred, *Tonal Pitch Space*. Cambridge: Cambridge University Press, 2001.

Lewin, David, "Behind the Beyond: A Response to Edward T. Cone," *Perspectives of New Music* 7/2(1969), pp. 59–69.

Lewin, David, "Music Theory, Phenomenology, and Modes of Perception," *Music Perception*, 3/4(1986), pp. 327–92.

Lodes, Birgit, "'When I try, now and then, to give musical form to my turbulent feelings': The Human and the Divine in the Gloria of Beethoven's *Missa solemnis*," *Beethoven Forum*, 6(1998), pp. 143–79.

Mathew, Nicholas, "History Under Erasure: *Wellingtons Sieg*, the Congress of Vienna, and the Ruination of Beethoven's Heroic Style," *Musical Quarterly* 89(2006), pp. 17–61.

Mathew, Nicholas, "Beethoven and his Others: Criticism, Difference, and the Composer's Many Voices," *Beethoven Forum*, 13(2006), pp. 148–87.

McClary, Susan, "Identity and Difference in Brahms's Third Symphony," in Ruth A. Solie (ed.), *Musicology and Difference. Gender and Sexuality in Music Scholarship*. Berkeley: University of California Press, 1993, pp. 326–44.

Meyer, Leonard B., *Style and Music: Theory, History, and Ideology*. Philadelphia: The University of Pennsylvania Press, 1989.

Nottebohm, Gustav, *Zweite Beethoveniana*. Leipzig, 1887.

Oster, Ernst, "The Dramatic Character of Beethoven's *Egmont* Overture," in David Beach (ed.), *Aspects of Schenkerian Theory*. New Haven: Yale University Press, 1983, pp. 209–22.

Ratner, Leonard G., *Classic Music: Expression, Form, and Style*. New York: Schirmer Books, 1980.

Ratz, Erwin, *Einführung in die musikalische Formenlehre: Über Formprinzipien in den Inventionen und Fugen J. S. Bachs und ihre Bedeutung für die Kompositionstechnik Beethovens* (3rd ed., enlarged). Vienna: Universal Edition, 1973.

Rosen, Charles, *The Classical Style*. New York: W. W. Norton, 1971.

Rosen, Charles, *Sonata Forms* (rev. ed.). New York: W. W. Norton, 1988.

Rothstein, William, *Phrase Rhythm in Tonal Music*. New York: Schirmer Books, 1989.

Rumph, Stephen, *Beethoven after Napoleon: Political Romanticism in the Late Works*. Berkeley: University of California Press, 2004.

Schachter, Carl, "Mozart's Last and Beethoven's First," in Cliff Eisen (ed.), *Mozart Studies*. New York: Oxford University Press, 1991, 227–251.

Schenker, Heinrich, *Free Composition* (trans. Ernst Oster). New York: Longman, 1979 [orig. published in German, 1935].

Schoenberg, Arnold, *Fundamentals of Musical Composition*, ed. Gerald Strang & Leonard Stein. London: Faber & Faber, 1967.

Schröter, Axel, *Musik zu den Schauspielen August von Kotzebues: Zur Bühnenpraxis während Goethes Leitung des Weimarer Hoftheaters*. Sinzig: Studio Verlag, 2006.

Sisman, Elaine, "Brahms's Slow Movements: Reinventing the 'Closed' Forms," in George S. Bozarth (ed.), *Brahms Studies: Analytical and Historical Perspectives*. Oxford: Clarendon, 1990, pp. 79–104.

Sisman, Elaine, *Mozart: The Jupiter Symphony*. Cambridge: Cambridge University Press, 1993.

Smith, Charles, "Musical Form and Fundamental Structure: An Investigation of Schenker's 'Formenlehre,'" *Music Analysis*, 15(1996), pp. 191–297.

Smith, Peter H., *Expressive Forms in Brahms's Instrumental Music*. Bloomington: Indiana University Press, 2005.

Spitzer, Michael, *Music as Philosophy: Adorno and Beethoven's Late Style*. Bloomington: Indiana University Press, 2006.

Steinbeck, Suzanne, *Die Ouvertüre in der Zeit von Beethoven bis Wagner: Probleme und Lösungen*. Munich: Emil Katzbichler, 1973.

Temperley, David, "End-Accented Phrases: An Analytical Exploration," *Journal of Music Theory*, 47(2003), pp. 125–54.

Tovey, Donald F., *Essays in Musical Analysis*, Vol. 1, London: Oxford University Press, 1935.

Tovey, Donald F., *Beethoven*. London: Oxford University Press, 1944.

Tovey, Donald F., *Musical Articles from the Encyclopaedia Britannica*. London: Oxford University Press, 1944.

Tovey, Donald F. "[Brahms:] Quartet in C Minor, Op. 60" (1901), repr. in Donald F. Tovey, *Essays in Musical Analysis: Chamber Music*. London: Oxford University Press, 1944, pp. 203–14.

Vallières, Michel, Daphne Tan, William E. Caplin, Joseph Shenker & Stephen McAdams, "Intrinsic Formal Functionality: Perception of Mozart's Materials," in Costas Tsougras & Richard Parncutt (eds.), *Proceedings of the Fourth Conference on Interdisciplinary Musicology* (Thessaloniki, Greece, 2–6 July 2008), http://web.auth.gr/cim08/.

Webster, James, "Schubert's Sonata Form and Brahms's First Maturity," *19th-Century Music*, 2(1977–78), pp. 1–35; 3 (1978–79), pp. 52–71.

Webster, James, "Brahms's *Tragic Overture*: The Form of Tragedy," in Robert Pascall (ed.), *Brahms: Biographical, Documentary and Analytical Studies*. Cambridge: Cambridge University Press, 1983, pp. 99–124.

Webster, James, *Haydn's* Farewell *Symphony and the Idea of Classical Style. Through-Composition and Cyclic Integration in His Instrumental Music*. Cambridge: Cambridge University Press, 1991.

Webster, James, "The Analysis of Mozart's Arias," in Cliff Eisen (ed.), *Mozart Studies*. New York: Oxford University Press, 1991, pp. 101–99.

Webster, James, "The Form of the Finale of Beethoven's Ninth Symphony," *Beethoven Forum*, 1(1992), pp. 25–62.

Webster, James, "Dahlhaus's *Beethoven* and the Ends of Analysis," *Beethoven Forum*, 2(1993), pp. 205–27.

Webster, James, (art.) "Sonata Form," *The New Grove* (rev. ed., 2001), Vol. 23, pp. 687–701.

Webster, James, "Haydn's Op. 9: A Critique of the Ideology of the 'Classical' String Quartet," in László Vikárius & Vera Lampert (eds.), *Essays in Honor of László Somfai on his 70th Birthday: Studies in the Sources and the Interpretation of Music* (Lanham, Maryland: Scarecrow Press, 2005), pp. 139–157.

Webster, James, "Rosen's Modernist Haydn," in Robert Curry et al. (eds.), *Variations on the Canon: Essays on Music from Bach to Boulez in Honor of Charles Rosen on his 80th Birthday*. Rochester: University of Rochester Press, 2008, pp. 283–90.

Westphal, Kurt, *Der Begriff der musikalischen Form in der Wiener Klassik: Versuch einer Grundlegung der Theorie der musikalischen Formung*. Leipzig: Breitkopf & Härtel, 1935 (2nd ed.: Giebig über Prien am Chiemsee: Katzbichler, 1971 (Schriften zur Musik, Vol. 11)).

About the Authors

William Caplin is James McGill Professor of Music Theory in the Schulich School of Music, McGill University (Montreal, Canada). His extensive investigations into formal procedures of late-eighteenth-century music culminated in the 1998 book *Classical Form: A Theory of Formal Functions for the Instrumental Music of Haydn, Mozart, and Beethoven* (Oxford University Press), which won the 1999 Wallace Berry Book Award from the Society for Music Theory. His article "The Classical Cadence: Conceptions and Misconceptions," published in the Spring 2004 issue of *The Journal of the American Musicological Society* was awarded the 2006 Prix Opus for Article of the Year from the Conseil québécois de la musique. Other studies on musical form have been published in *Eighteenth-Century Music*, *Beethoven Forum*, *Musiktheorie*, *The Journal of Musicological Research*, *Tijdschrift voor Muziektheorie*, and *Beethoven's Compositional Process* (ed. William Kinderman). Caplin was elected to a two-year term as President of the Society for Music Theory beginning November 2005. He co-chaired the 2004 Mannes Institute of Advanced Theoretical Studies, where he led a workshop on "Exposition Structure in Beethoven's Piano Sonatas: A Form-Functional Approach." Caplin serves on the editorial boards of *Eighteenth-Century Music* and *Eastman Studies in Music*.

James Hepokoski is Professor of Music at Yale University. Combining aspects of musicology and music theory with issues of European and American methodological practice and cultural theory, his areas of specialization range broadly in musical topics from ca. 1750 to ca. 1950. These include close studies of historical contexts and genres, formal structural types, and diverse concepts of analysis and hermeneutics; symphonic and chamber works from Haydn, Mozart, and Beethoven through Mahler, Sibelius, Elgar, and Richard Strauss; sonata-form theory and sonata deformations; conceptions of musical modernism, ca. 1880-1920; music, ideology, nationalism, and cultural identity; Italian opera (Verdi, Puccini); and the interplays of differing music traditions in the United States, 1900-1950. He was a co-editor of the musicological journal *19-Century Music* from 1992 to 2005. He is the author of five books and numerous articles on a wide variety of topics. In collaboration with Warren Darcy (Oberlin College Conservatory), Hepokoski has developed a new, genre-based mode of sonata-form analysis—Sonata Theory—that merges historical research, current music theory, and recent styles of textual questioning and interpretation (*Elements of Sonata Theory. Norms, Types and Deformations in Late-Eighteenth-Century Sonata* – Oxford University Press, 2006; winner of the 2008 Wallace Berry Book Award from the Society of Music Theory). A selection of his writings, *Music, Structure, Thought*, is forthcoming from Ashgate in 2009.

JAMES WEBSTER is the Goldwin Smith Professor of Music at Cornell University. He specializes in the history and theory of music of the eighteenth and nineteenth centuries, with a particular focus on Haydn (cf. *Haydn's* Farewell *Symphony and the Idea of Classical Style: Through-Composition and Cyclic Integration in His Instrumental Music* – Cambridge University Press, 1991 – and *The New Grove Haydn* – Palgrave/Macmillan, 2002). His other interests include Mozart (especially his operas), Beethoven, Schubert, and Brahms, as well as performance practice, editorial practice, and the historiography of music; in music theory he specializes in issues of musical form (including analytical methodology) and Schenkerian analysis. He was a founding editor of the journal *Beethoven Forum*, and was a musicological consultant for the recordings of Haydn's symphonies on original instruments, by the Academy of Ancient Music under Christopher Hogwood (Decca/L'Oiseau-lyre). Among the many honors he has received are the Einstein and Kinkeldey Awards of the American Musicological Society, a Fulbright dissertation grant, two Senior Research Fellowships from the National Endowment for the Humanities, a Guggenheim Fellowship, and a Research Fellowship of the Alexander von Humboldt Foundation (Germany). He served as President of the American Musicological Society. He is a Fellow of the American Academy of Arts and Sciences and a member of the Executive Committee of the Board of Directors of the Joseph Haydn Institute.

Pieter Bergé is professor of music history, analysis and music theory at the University of Leuven, Belgium. His main research areas are the formal analysis of classical and early romantic music, German opera in the first half of the twentieth century, and music analysis and performance. He has published two monographs on the operas of Arnold Schoenberg—*De Eenheid in het Dualisme: Idee en Representatie in Schönbergs Opera* Moses und Aron (2002) and *Arnold Schönberg en de Zeitoper* (2006). He is the author of numerous articles on topics related to music aesthetics, opera history and formal analysis (*Journal of the Arnold Schoenberg Center*, *Musiktheorie*, *Perspectives of New Music*, *Dutch Journal for Music Theory*, *Revue Belge de Musicologie*, and others). Bergé is editor of a collection of essays offering twelve different analytical interpretations of Beethoven's *Tempest Sonata* that will appear in 2009 (*Beethoven's* Tempest *Sonata: Perspectives of Analysis and Performance*; co-edited by William E. Caplin and Jeroen D'hoe). He was a fellow of the Mannes Institute of Advanced Theoretical Studies in 2004 ('Musical Form') and 2007 ('Arnold Schoenberg and his Legacy'). He was appointed President of the Dutch-Flemish Society for Music Theory in 2006. He is a member of the editorial board of the series *Analysis in Context: Leuven Studies in Musicology*.

CPSIA information can be obtained
at www.ICGtesting.com
Printed in the USA
LVOW13s2153240117
522012LV00014B/346/P